As the time comes when you no longer wish to see
what I previously desired,
when instead your will is what you wanted,
it is then that you purify me.

But where has my freedom been
for so long?
From what secret depths was it dragged out
in an instant
that I might agree to bow my head
beneath your yoke which is gentle
and accept on my shoulders your burden
which is light,
O Lord Jesus Christ,
my strength and my redeemer?

How suddenly comforting it was
to lose the false comforts of the past!
I had long feared losing them,
and now it was a joy to throw them away.

Truly it was you who put them far from me,
my true and supreme comfort;
you put them far away
and set yourself in their place.

ST. AUGUSTINE
THE CONFESSIONS 9.1

WHEN GOD INTERRUPTS

FINDING NEW LIFE THROUGH UNWANTED CHANGE

M. CRAIG BARNES

InterVarsity Press
Downers Grove, Illinois

InterVarsity Press® is the book-publishing division of InterVarsity Christian Fellowship®, a student movement active on campus at hundreds of universities, colleges and schools of nursing in the United States of America, and a member movement of the International Fellowship of Evangelical Students. For information about local and regional activities, write Public Relations Dept., InterVarsity Christian Fellowship, 6400 Schroeder Rd., P.O. Box 7895, Madison, WI 53707-7895.

Scripture quotations, unless otherwise noted, are from the New Revised Standard Version of the Bible, copyright 1989 by the Division of Christian Education of the National Council of the Churches of Christ in the USA. Used by permission. All rights reserved.

Cover illustration: Roberta Polfus

ISBN 0-8308-1979-7
Printed in the United States of America ∞

Library of Congress Cataloging-in-Publication Data

Barnes, M. Craig.
   When God interrupts: finding new life through unwanted change/
  M. Craig Barnes.
     p.   cm.
   Includes bibliographical references.
   ISBN 0-8308-1979-7 (pbk.: alk. paper)
   1. Life change events—Religious aspects—Christianity. 2. Loss
(Psychology)—Religious aspects—Christianity. 3. Consolation.
4. Conversion. I. Title.
BV4908.5.B36   1996
248.8'6—dc20   95-50979
                                    CIP

| 17 | 16 | 15 | 14 | 13 | 12 | 11 | 10 | 9 | 8 | 7 | 6 | 5 | | | |
| 10 | 09 | 08 | 07 | 06 | 05 | 04 | 03 | 02 | 01 | 00 | 99 | 98 | 97 | | |

*In honor of
my father and my mother*

Introduction

We just keep losing things: wives, husbands, friends, health, the dreams and security of the past. Nothing stays the way it was.

I have yet to meet an adult who is living the life he or she planned. Some are thrilled about that: "Thank God life turned out so much better than I had hoped." Seldom does a week go by, though, that I don't meet as a pastor with those who are a long way from thanking God for a loss of what was cherished. Nobody wants to be abandoned.

Typically, those who consider themselves abandoned were deserted by something or someone they needed. A wife comes home to find a note on the refrigerator: "I'm leaving you." An employee of twenty years walks into his boss's office to be told he is being laid off that day. A young woman undergoes a mastectomy and wonders if she will ever stop crying. These people had counted on a spouse or a career or at least their health. One day these things are gone, and life will never again be the same.

In the course of life, we expect to suffer some necessary losses. Children grow up and leave home. A new job in a different town forces us to say goodby to friends and family in the place we have to leave. Eventually, one aged spouse places the other in the arms of God. Some abandonments we can count on, but that does not mean they are less painful.

One of the most heroic things people do is voluntarily leave their comfortable dissatisfactions with life in order to receive the new opportunity they hope is waiting around the corner. When that happens, their experience may not be filled with the pathos of those who are deserted, but their abandoned journey through fear and grief into the new life is no less dramatic.

However it comes, abandonment can always be embraced as the opportunity to receive a new life. A devastated widow can outlive her grief. A hurt, disappointed divorcé eventually picks up the broken pieces and begins again. A lost job can become the beginning of a new vocation.

Making the choice to accept abandonment as the opportunity to discover a new life is hard. It is as great a challenge as life ever presents us. Yet this is an absolutely central dynamic to the Christian life.

If we are planning on spending very much time following Jesus Christ, we can count on a great deal of abandonment. He kept trying to tell that to his disciples. Jesus was constantly saying things like "Only those who lose their lives will find them."

We have a name for this process in the Christian church. We call it *conversion*.

That is what this book is about. It is about the stories of men and women in the Bible, as well as those in the congregation I serve, who have discovered they are not living the life they had planned. Each of them has faced significant loss. Something that they once held dear has been taken away, and that has forced them to make a frightening choice. Will they clutch at something else for their salvation? Or can they leave their hands open long enough to receive the life Jesus was dying to give them?

1
Losing Our Lives

OUR EXPERIENCES WITH ABANDONMENT and unwanted change are crisis moments when we must decide whether or not to leave behind the life that is gone forever. We can do that only if we believe in the ongoing creativity of God, who brings light and beauty to the dark chaos of our losses in life.

For All the Saints

The phone rang at 11 a.m. on Thanksgiving. I hesitated before answering it because I knew it could mean an interruption in our plans for the day. I was right. A nurse was calling from the intensive care ward. "Pastor Barnes, Jean Bonfield had another heart attack. It looks like she's dying."

Jean, age seventy-eight, was a member of my congregation. She and her husband, Bill, always sat in the third pew, right-hand side. She had taught Sunday school for over thirty-five years and quit only after her sight failed. Since then she had settled into a ministry of prayer.

When I arrived at the hospital, the family members were standing in a circle around her bed. I went into her room, took her hand and said, "Jean, it's Craig. Can I pray for you?" She smiled softly.

I had visited Jean in the hospital on several occasions. Praying for her was like asking God to give more faith to the apostle Paul. Jean believed in the grace of God. She believed that in Jesus Christ her sins were forgiven, and she believed she would live eternally with him when she died. She never understood my sermons about "I believe, help my unbelief." Jean had very little unbelief.

Beside her bed, I started to read some Scripture passages. I would start reading, and she would finish the passage, quoting it from memory. Her voice was weak, but her mind seemed strong even through the fog of the pain-deadening morphine. Someone whispered it was a shame that she was dying on Thanksgiving. But Jean responded, "What a glorious Thanksgiving. Soon I'll be with my Lord. I'm almost there."

Then she began to pray. She prayed for everyone around the bed: her husband, her children and her grandchildren. She even prayed for her pastor. She asked God to help me believe the words of my own sermons. Shortly after her prayer, Jean died. As we watched the lines that measured her vital signs level out on the monitor, the room was overcome by a quiet spirit. It was a sacred moment, and no one dared defile it by trying to say something meaningful. Jean was passing from our hands into God's.

After she was gone, we each took a moment beside her to say goodby. Then we held hands and began to pray again. In the middle of my prayer I discovered that I was already missing her very much. Someone else had to finish my prayer.

As I drove away from the hospital, it occurred to me for the first time that Jean was a saint. An ordinary and unadorned one, but clearly a saint whose clarity of faith and vision made it easier for me to believe. What I was missing was not just a favorite parishioner, but one of my windows into heaven.

I was very late for the Thanksgiving dinner party. When I walked through the door, I could hear my friends laughing at the table. At first I wondered if I was ready for this. One of the hardest things about being a pastor is the transitions. My heart never moves as fast as the schedule of events. But to my surprise, this transition was easy. Jean made it easy. I sat down at the table and simply said, "What a glorious Thanksgiving!"

I find that people die pretty much the way they live. We have all heard about deathbed confessions, but I've never witnessed one. What I've seen at the end of someone's life reflects what was always typical of that person. Those who live most of their lives in fear are usually petrified of dying. Those who always have friends seldom die alone. Those who value prayer want to pray at the end.

But Jean Bonfield, with her simple, unquestioning faith, is not the only model of the Christian life. Quite frankly, I can't imagine having unquestioning belief, and I don't even aspire to it. I bristle at easy answers that jump to the lips before the question is formed, too soon to be certain that it is the right question, too soon to hear the pathos and the deep sighs of the heart that lie behind someone's doubts. In fact, I have discovered that doubt is but one more door to deeper faith in the grace of God.

But I hope to end my days as one who has lived as a Christian. I do want to get this right. Legions of Sunday-school teachers and camp counselors planted within my childhood heart an enduring hope to one day greet Christ and hear him say, "Well done, thou good and faithful servant."

Faith does not come easily for me. "Praise the Lord" is not

the first thing I find myself saying in times of tragedy. But I too am on a spiritual journey following Jesus Christ, even though I seem to drag my doubts behind me. And I do hope through all the detours, confusion and half-truths of my life, that I'll eventually end my days like Jean—as one of "the saints who from their labors rest."

Jean Bonfield had as good a death as I have seen. It was clear that she died as she had lived, with faith and love. The question I have often asked since that day is, How did she get there? Saints aren't born. They are made along the way.

Saint-Making

We pastors spend some of our time with the dying, but we spend most of our schedule with those who are quietly making their way through the ambiguity of daily life. We see lives that are still being created. We are invited to witness what Episcopal priest Alan Jones has called the "unfinishedness of human existence."[1]

What is unfinished is the high drama of Jesus' next invitation and my parishioner's next choice. Will this man become Peter, who drops everything to follow Jesus until he discovers that there is no longer an old life waiting for him? Or will this would-be disciple respond like the rich young ruler, who, when confronted with the cost of following Jesus, returned sadly to the life he could not leave?

Saints know what it means to lose their lives in following Jesus. They also know that they find life in losing it. Whether it is St. Peter or St. Jean Bonfield, the cost of their veneration is high—higher than they ever could have imagined. Had they known the cost going into this deal with God, they would have certainly backed out.

On the other side of it all, on a deathbed, any saint will tell you about "a glorious thanksgiving." But as one who has the high honor of walking alongside saints in the making, I have become convinced that Christianity is fundamentally an experience in losing the lives of our dreams in order to receive the lives Jesus died to give us.

Those who would bear the name *Christian* credibly experience a tremendous amount of abandonment in life. The Savior made that painfully clear:

As they were going along the road, someone said to him, "I will follow you wherever you go." And Jesus said to him, "Foxes have holes, and birds of the air have nests; but the Son of Man has nowhere to lay his head." To another he said, "Follow me." But he said, "Lord, first let me go and bury my father." But Jesus said to him, "Let the dead bury their own dead; but as for you, go and proclaim the kingdom of God." Another said, "I will follow you, Lord; but let me first say farewell to those at my home." Jesus said to him, "No one who puts a hand to the plow and looks back is fit for the kingdom of God." (Luke 9:57-62)

I spent the first years of my pastorate trying to soften these verses. "Well, Jesus didn't literally mean you have to leave everything and everyone behind. He just meant you had to be willing to do so." But I no longer say things like that to my congregation. To provide them with an escape from Jesus' clear teaching is not the good news I once thought it was.

The good news I have for them is that Jesus is their *only* hope. If Christians are truly willing to leave everything to follow him, then they will, in fact, eventually leave everything. Either voluntarily or involuntarily, either by design or by accident, a day will come when they realize they have only Jesus. If he alone is savior, then we can find our lives only in being his disciples.

We have to abandon all hope that we can hang on to any other dream, any other relationship, any other vocation. For most of us this is asking too much. Given the choice between selling everything to blindly follow Jesus or returning sadly to our old life, we will choose the latter every time. That is why grace often comes in severe ways. We really don't have to seek abandonment. It finds us easily enough. Usually it comes as God's uninvited angel with the announcement of "good news" that we are about to lose our lives. In one way or another most of us have met that angel. The question is, Can we lean into the abandonment? Can we accept it as the Savior's invitation to find our lives at long last?

We will probably spend most of life with family, friends, good health and good work. But they are not ours by rights. They are not promised to us. We may have to give them back to God at any moment. Someday we will give them back. The trick is to learn how to do that before they leave us. That allows us to spend the rest of our time enjoying them as the temporary gifts that they are.

An Age of Abandonment
We are living in a society where confusion and loss have replaced certainty and security. Social commentators describe our time in history as "postmodern." That means ours is a day known not for its creativity, but for the abandonment of earlier hopes. The promises on which modern society rested—education, progress, reason, the innate goodness of humanity, the family, science and technology—have all proven to be more limited than we had once thought. Today the arts, literature, architecture and even theology are often focused on the deconstruction of this modern world.

According to a recent Gallup survey, two out of three Americans believe the United States is in a serious long-term decline that is economic, moral and spiritual. According to one businessman who was questioned,

The issues that are now on people's minds are not coffee table-talk. They are gut wrenching issues that make us lie in bed wide awake, and stare at the ceiling, and wonder what are we leaving for our children? And what are we building for ourselves?[2]

On issue after issue—crime, the economy, health care, poverty and homelessness—the vast majority believe we are losing ground. Seventy-three percent of us believe our children will be prevented from attaining as high a standard of living as we have.

The marriage rate has fallen 25 percent since 1960, while the divorce rate has doubled and the percentage of families headed by a single parent has tripled. According to some projections, only 30 percent of white children born in 1980 will live with both parents through age eighteen.[3] It is clear that we are not returning to the world of Ozzie and Harriet. Too many of us have been abandoned by that dream.

Abandonment has become a permanent social dynamic that is feeding off itself. As children of broken homes grow older, they find it difficult to trust commitments and frequently sabotage them out of fear. Some never get close enough to be hurt. Others just make sure they always leave first.

In the church I get to see this social and economic breakdown firsthand, with names and faces attached. These are not just "issues":

☐ A couple spent thirty years working hard, paying off a mortgage, being good neighbors, singing in the church choir. Then one morning one of them walks out the door and decides not to come back.

☐ A man in surgery receives a blood transfusion. The blood was tainted, and this father of four now has AIDS. The doctors say they are sorry.

☐ A woman is called into her supervisor's office. He explains about corporate downsizing for the recession. Her job has been terminated. He hopes that she will understand. She goes back to her office. She packs up her hopes for getting ahead. She wonders what she will tell her kids.

Nothing is nailed down. We have been abandoned by the dreams our parents gave us. Those dreams would come true, we were told, if only we worked hard. We now find the world too arbitrary and too unjust to believe in the dreams. We feel abandoned, even betrayed, by many of our great social accomplishments.

In his book *Hope in Time of Abandonment* Jacques Ellul has traced the tragic ironies of this age. We live in one of the most pacified and peaceful times in history, but we feel personal insecurity ever more acutely. While living in one of the most scientific and technologically advanced societies, we act more irrationally in personal relationships. While living in one of the most mobile of societies, we find life more inflexible. While living in one of the most liberal of the free societies, we are flocking to therapists to deal with our compulsive behavior patterns.[4] For many, the best narcotic to deal with this malaise is shopping for more things. But the narcotic wears off, and we soon need more. Despite being the wealthiest society in history, we are up to our ears in debt.

A strange determinism seems to be pulling control out of our hands. Never before have we had such means to make our own history, yet we still complain about the mythic "they" who are to blame for our problems.

Arising in the midst of all this decline are the demonic forces of racism and greed. When the days of American prosperity have receded and the American pie is no longer growing, people tend to get more obsessed with their slice. We begin to listen to those who warn us that someone is out to steal our lifestyle. The demons of racism and greed are not simply social forces. They find their power in our hearts. They make their way into our homes. They make us afraid to send our kids to public schools. They make us keep an eye on who bought that vacant house down the street. They make us abandon our contemporary prophets who had a dream for all of us.

This creates new challenges for those who want to speak to people in ways that are culturally relevant and biblically faithful. In the past we explained how Christians can know God with certainty. In the future we will need to maintain faith in God in the midst of serious doubts that anything is certain.

The church must learn how to hear the haunting questions that are being asked in public speeches and editorials. More often they are asked off-stage, late at night, when people can't get to sleep. Once we hear these contemporary questions, we rush to the Bible to buttress our causes and our dreams. But in it we read about a messiah who has some very different ideas about salvation. Jesus refused to relieve the people's anxieties about the Roman issue, or the tax issue, or the issues of health, hunger or religion. Instead, he invited people further into their fears. It was the only way they could find a savior.

A Thesis on Abandoned Faith

As I have accompanied my parishioners into the discovery of what it means that Jesus is their Savior, I have observed that they always experience the light of hope at the point where they succumb to their darkest fear. Jesus put it better when he said, "Those who want to save their life will lose it, and those who lose their life for my sake will save it" (Luke 9:24).

It is impossible to follow Jesus and not be led away from something. That journey away from the former places and toward the new place is what converts us. Conversion is not simply the acceptance of a theological formula for eternal salvation. Of course it is that, but it is so much more. It is the discovery of God's painful, beautiful, ongoing creativity along the way in our lives.

It was this converting activity of God that turned a Hebrew fugitive into the liberator of Israel, a boy shepherd into a king, fishermen into fishers of men, a Jewish persecutor of the church into the apostle to the Gentiles. It raised the dead Lazarus to be the living friend of Jesus who ate and communed with him.

In every biblical illustration of conversion, there is a mission attached. No one is converted for exclusively personal benefit. This may be why we have to lose our lives in order to find them. The purpose of conversion in the Bible is not our spiritual self-actualization but Christ's mission. The drama of biblical conversion is never limited to the safe struggle between doubt and belief in Christian doctrines. Rather, it always involves the extraordinary process of creating visionary apostles out of fearful disciples.

That is what I know about. I write, preach and teach about it because it is what I see God doing in the lives of those I love. These are ordinary Christians, distinctive only because their typical losses have led them into new missions. They thought their cancer or their divorce or their grief meant the end of their lives. They were right. Life as they knew it was over. In its place they were given not just a new life, but a new purpose to life.

In the church we refer to someone's mission in life as a Christian vocation. One may or may not get paid for this. It may or may not be considered work. Some vocations are focused more on maintaining relationships. Other vocations are focused on completing tasks. Some vocations the church easily honors, like those we ordain to be deacons, elders and pastors. Other vocations we haven't figured out how to ordain, like those who are salt and light in the marketplace, those who take care of the big needs of small children at home, and those who are called to a ministry of prayer.

The word _vocation_ comes from the Latin _vocarie,_ which simply means to call. Your vocation is your calling. It is what God has asked to do with your life. People usually know it when they have one. And they always know it when they don't.

If Christian vocation is about what you are called to do, Christian conversion is about what you are called to be. You can't have one without the other. The church has a tendency to call people first to conversion. Later it gets around to their responsibility to help out with missions. But in the Bible we find men and women who were being constantly converted by their vocations: Abraham, Moses, David, Elijah, Paul and the disciples of Christ. It was the call that converted them. There was no way for them to receive these life-changing vocations, however, without first abandoning, or being abandoned by, all hope in their former life.

As Jesus prophesied to Peter, our vocation is to a place "where you do not wish to go" (John 21:18). In part that is because we do not want to abandon the place where we have been trying to save our own lives. But the main reason we don't want to go to the place Christ would call us is that we know that we will have to abandon our most cherished images of who we are.

Give Me That Old Time Religion

When I was thirteen years old, the Eastern Valley Boys came to our town. They were a singing-preaching quartet who had been invited to lead a week of revival services. They wore matching green blazers and had lots of teeth that gleamed when they sang. Somehow they made "The Old Rugged Cross" dance with their enthusiasm.

Their performance was helped tremendously by the gigantic

three-pole tent that been rented for the revival. The smell of sawdust and wet canvas, the neatly arranged rows of folded chairs, the rough sounds of an old amplifier system turned too high, the string of naked light bulbs draped across the tent poles all created an atmosphere of earthy spirituality.

No one knew or cared much about the education of our revival preachers. At the meetings—they were never called worship—there were no creeds, vestments or even bulletins. The volunteer choir, made up mostly of overweight women, wouldn't sing anything written by J. S. Bach. But I knew they were good for at least ten verses of "Just As I Am" at the end of the evening.

As a young boy, I was entranced by all of this. The big tent created a doorway from our blue-collar world to a completely different life. Despite its circus atmosphere, the tent invited us to encounter something completely different from the world we knew.

I sat next to my childhood friends. We did not consider ourselves poor, but it would be generous to call some of our parents blue-collar. Many of them were out of work altogether, having gone from job to job. Alcohol abuse was a big problem, as probably was wife abuse, but no one talked much about that. We had seen our parents endure almost every abandonment under the sun. Had we dared to talk about it, we would have admitted that the American dream had long ago left our town. Even a thirteen-year-old boy could tell that this kind of life wasn't what God had in mind.

Everything that happened on those hot nights led to the preacher's invitation at the end of the evening. As the choir hummed softly in the background, he urged us, again and again, to step out, walk forward and give our lives to Jesus. This was the moment. Now was the time to turn away from the disappointments of the world and turn to the Savior.

It has been a long time since I sat in a tent revival. I have now collected far too many theological degrees and have committed myself to a theological tradition that would be aghast at just about everything that went on in the old tent. I can count the blue collars in my Presbyterian church on one hand. I have actually become quite fond of J. S. Bach. and even more committed to the pipe organ whose music fills our very large marble sanctuary. I love liturgy, and if I don't get a good Kyrie or Sanctus out of our chancel choir at Holy Communion I feel robbed. But sometimes, when I am singing in the shower, I catch myself about halfway through "The Old Rugged Cross."

In the course of my religious career, it would have been easy to dismiss, or at least try to hide, my early experiences with the revivals. It would not be hard to challenge much of the theology of the Eastern Valley Boys, assuming they had one. I seriously doubt that I could now remain in their tent very long. But I cannot escape the memory of their invitation—"Now is the opportunity to step out, walk forward and give your life to God." I still think they were quite right about that.

Today as a pastor, I speak to people who seem to be very different from those who fanned themselves in the revival tent on hot summer nights. They dress up a little better, make a lot more money and in general have done pretty well by the American dream. But every Sunday I look into the pews and see people who have been abandoned by family, health and fulfillment at work.

I see successful women who are turning forty and wondering why they aren't married with children. I see women who have given up their careers to stay home with children and wonder if the world is passing them by.

We have a church filled with men in their fifties who are not happy about what they do for a living. But they can't afford to quit their jobs because they need them to afford a lifestyle they really don't like.

In worship every Sunday there are parents sitting next to kids whom they don't understand but do worry about. Filled with anxiety, these parents say and do desperate things that push the kids into even stonier silence.

For every wedding I perform, there are at least two marriages that are on the rocks in our church. Every time I baptize a new baby, I always seem to catch the eye of a new widow who is still trying to figure out how she will go on in life without her beloved.

I see all of this every single Sunday in church. I see it all week long in hospitals, living rooms, company cafeterias and my own office. Like the thirteen-year-old boy who once sat in the old revival tent, I know this isn't what God had in mind. Like the revivalists before me, I try to create a doorway between heaven and earth. I say to these Christians I love so much, "Now would be a good opportunity to step out, walk forward and give your life to Jesus."

Of course, they did that long ago, maybe in confirmation class or on a youth retreat. Or maybe they have just grown up believing in Jesus. But now they have to trust him. Now they have been abandoned by all the other saviors. Now they have to let the dead bury the dead, put their hands to the plow and not look back.

Conversion Aversion

There is some aversion, even in evangelical circles, to talking too much about conversion. Maybe it is because we are embarrassed by the fiery preachers among us whose angry rhetoric melts away any words of true grace and love. Maybe it is because we have been around converted people long enough to realize that there isn't much that's really different about them. Maybe it's because we have grown tired of evangelists who count up conversions but have little to say about those who are hungry, homeless, sick, naked or in prison (Matthew 25:43). We all know there is more to the gospel than getting people to sign decision cards.

But these are not the best reasons for being timid about conversion. The best reason is that it will change everything. Conversion is central to both the Old and New Testaments. You can't get through the teachings of the prophets, the apostles or Jesus himself without encountering the invitation to let go of the life that is taking you nowhere, abandon your abandonments—step out, walk forward and give your life to God. Who knows what he might do with it?

The very word *conversion* sends the emotions flying. Some hear it and immediately think of warm memories when God entered their life. They remember the exact time and place. They want others to have the same experience. In fact, they feel compelled by Scripture to make sure that others have exactly the same experience. But when some others hear the word, they want to run out of the room. It is not just the non-Christian who reacts this way. So do those who, like Timothy, were raised in the "lap of faith." These cannot remember the specific time and place they began to believe in Jesus as Savicr, any more then they can remember the time they believed in the love of their parents.

Debate about how one gets converted has gone on for a long time. It is linked to competing perspectives on baptism, evangelism and the nature of the church. That debate is very important, but we only scratch the surface of the doctrine of conversion if we limit it to a discussion of when the life of a Christian believer begins.

Conversion describes a lot more of the Christian journey than its initiation. It also describes what happens to those who stay on the road behind Jesus, as he takes them to a place they would rather not go and gives them a vocation that changes everything.

The Invitation

Central to the Bible's teaching on conversion is the call to make a choice. Confronted with abandonment, Christians can either turn their hearts back to the things they lost or turn toward the hope that Jesus Christ is in fact their Savior.

The theological term for this choice is repentance. The Greek word for repentance is _metanoia_. It simply means "to turn." Before it became a biblical term, _metanoia_ was commonly used to describe the process of turning around. If a man left the house and then remembered he had forgotten something, he would "repent," turn around and go back home. Over the centuries, the church endowed the word with connotations of judgment and remorse. But the biblical call to repent and be converted still essentially means to turn toward the work God is doing in our lives.

Life continues to confront Christians with invitations to repent and be converted, even after we have begun to turn our faces toward God. Our eternal salvation may be secured by the initial decision to accept Christ's forgiveness, but conversion is the lifelong process of turning away from our plans and turning toward God's maddening, disruptive creativity.

In spite of all our carefulness and hard work, we probably will not achieve the life of our dreams. In fact, our dreams are precisely the things that have abandoned us. But it is then that we hear the invitation of Jesus Christ, "Now is the opportunity to step out, walk forward and give your life to God."

2
Terrifying Opportunity

CONVERSION COMES ALWAYS AS GOD'S idea, not our own. It scares us. Since God is the initiator, conversion is a grace— a grace that scares us too much.

Converting the Religious

Most of my parishioners would have liked the apostle Paul before he got converted. He was hardworking, ambitious and very committed to his religious values. Saul, as he was called then, was the fulfillment of every Jewish mother's wildest dreams.

He had a good job with the system. Basically, it was his job to make sure that nothing changed. The biggest threat to that control was a new Jewish cult called "The Way." Some forty years later it came to be called Christianity. Those who belonged to The Way were followers of a carpenter named Jesus, now dead, who had once claimed to be the Messiah. The heretics insisted that he had risen from the dead and that he was the hope of the world.

Saul hated these new religious ideas. Why would someone threaten the wonderful, time-honored, theologically sophisticated traditions? The only thing Saul wanted changed was anything that threatened his understanding of God. Saul knew all about God, and he wasn't about to abandon his corner on the truth.

He received word that some adherents of The Way were hiding in Damascus. So he set out to track them down. Along the road, *en route to doing so much good for God,* Saul was blinded by a light brighter than the sun. He fell to the ground and heard a voice saying, "Saul, Saul, why do you persecute me?" There was more to God than Saul knew.

Notice, this was not the conversion of the penitent sinner. Saul did not come to God asking forgiveness. In fact, this conversion wasn't even Saul's idea. Conversion always begins as God's terrifying initiative in our lives.

It scares us to think that God would actually intervene in our good lives and say, "I don't care how devoutly you believe, you don't know who I am." If that happened, life would be very different. The inverse of that is also true. No matter how desperately we may want to change, we never will unless we see God differently. God alone is the Converter. We cannot change ourselves, and we cannot help but be changed when he reveals more of himself to us.

To follow Jesus is to enter the lifelong process of discovering more about God than we know, discovering that "my ways are not your ways," discovering that we have been worshiping not God but an expectation of God. Nothing makes it harder to see God than our expectations of him. They blind us to the new ways he is at work saving our lives. Conversion pulls us away from being religious, away from having all the answers. It turns us into pilgrims who journey through life with some hard questions. For God is always working just beyond our limits, inviting us to venture into the unknown where we are abandoned by everything—especially by our prior expectations of God.

Once Saul gained this greater vision of the Lord, he was transformed from being the persecutor of the church into its leading proponent.

Saul's personality did not change all that much. But the zeal that formerly persecuted the church became the zeal that took the gospel around the world. Eventually his name was changed to its Hellenized version—Paul. With that change it was clear that his Jewish identity had been converted by his new mission to the Gentiles. Again, it's the mission that does the converting.

About the time Paul was receiving his vision from the Lord, Ananias, an elder of the new church, also received a vision. He was told to go to the house of Judas and care for Paul. At first Ananias was hesitant to care for this persecutor, but the Lord insisted, and so the elder got converted as well. Paul's conversion was to the church. Ananias's conversion was back to the world from which the church had been hiding.

God reassured the church that Paul was "an instrument whom I have chosen to bring my name before Gentiles and kings and before the people of Israel; I myself will show him how much he must suffer for the sake of my name" (Acts 9:15). There it is. He was converted because he was an instrument of the Lord. The benefit of this conversion was that he would suffer for the Lord. At the end of his career, Paul told the Philippians that he counts "everything a loss compared to the surpassing greatness of knowing Christ Jesus my Lord" (Philippians 3:7 NIV). Sooner or later, everything else is abandoned for the sake of the only one we will never lose.

It is significant that Paul died while the church was still

young and struggling. While he sat in the Roman jail, he must have had moments of deep doubt, wondering if the Christian mission would survive. This is another illustration of the fact that conversion has purposes that far exceed its benefits to the individual. We are converted to a great mission that outlives us. We now work for the coming kingdom of Jesus Christ that was on the way before we arrived and will continue to come long after we are gone. In familiar words of St. Augustine, "Nothing worth doing can be accomplished in one's lifetime."

Converting the Religious—Another Story

Shortly before my seventeenth birthday, my brother and I came home from the Christian camps where we had been working for the summer to learn that our mom and dad were divorcing. Mom had already left him. Dad resigned from the church where he was pastor, and then he left—everyone. We still don't know where he is.

Maybe Dad's sense of failure was so great that he couldn't see his sons without anguishing over the family that was lost. Maybe leaving us was easy. We'll never know. He has missed the things that are important to most fathers—graduations, weddings, career choices, grandchildren. For a while my brother and I tried hard to find him, but in time we learned to let him go.

I know about abandonment. I know that you never really get over it. I also know it can force changes that you think will kill you, but in fact they save your life.

The Christmas after our parents split up, my brother and I wanted to visit Mom. We didn't have enough money for a bus, so we decided to hitchhike. If the rides went well, we figured we could make it in a couple of days. The rides did not go well. It got dark. It began to snow. There were fewer and fewer cars on the expressway.

When we were young, my father had forced us to memorize Scripture. I could never quite understand the purpose of it, since there seemed little threat that the "godless communists" were going to take away our Bibles. But we would often get quizzed on our verses. Dad would toss out a Bible reference, and we would have to recite the text. I did it because I was told it was important, because everyone I admired in our small church did it, because I was sure God himself wanted me to memorize Scripture. But mostly I did it because I had to. As the years piled up, so did the verses I had memorized. I had God tucked away in the corners of my mind. Just give me the reference, and I could reproduce him for anyone.

Standing on the side of that road, as the night got darker and the snow fell harder, my brother and I started talking about what in the world had happened to us. After a while we couldn't really talk about it anymore. To keep our minds off the cold, to remind us of our lost home, we started quizzing each other on memory verses. Back and forth we went:

Trust in the LORD with all your heart,
and do not rely on your own insight.
In all your ways acknowledge him,
and he will make straight your paths. (Proverbs 3:5)
We know that all things work together for good
for those who love God,
who are called according to his purpose. (Romans 8:28)
For surely I know the plans I have for you, says the LORD,
plans for your welfare and not for harm,
to give you a future with hope. (Jeremiah 29:11)
Do not fear, for I have redeemed you;
I have called you by name, you are mine.
When you pass through the waters, I will be with you;
and through the rivers, they shall not overwhelm you;
when you walk through the fire you shall not be burned,

and the flame shall not consume you.
For I am the LORD your God,
    the Holy One of Israel, your Savior.
I give Egypt as your ransom,
    Ethiopia and Seba in exchange for you.
Because you are precious in my sight,
    and honored, and I love you. (Isaiah 43:1-4)

That night for the first time in my life I heard those verses, maybe because I was ready to hear them. I was confused, frightened and grieving over the loss of everything that had once held my world together. I needed a savior.

Was that a conversion experience? Of course. Not the first one. Certainly not the last one. But it allowed me to step out, walk forward and give more of my life to Jesus. What else was I going to do with it? That is the great advantage of abandonment—it makes it easier to hear God's words of love and purpose for us.

For Paul it happened on the Damascus road. For me it happened on Interstate 81. I saw no blinding light, but I did discover that there was more to God than I knew. Through my Sunday-school classes, my Christian home, my youth group and my memorized verses, I thought I had captured God like a canary in my hand. But when I opened my hand, all I found was a Bible reference. Now I had to believe. I had to believe not in what I knew about God, because that was just information. Now I had to believe that God knew me. I had to believe that I was precious, honored and loved.

I did not receive my call to the pastoral ministry that night. That would come much later through my fumbling efforts as a seminary intern. But I did receive a call to usefulness. I began that evening as a lost teenager on the side of the road. After hearing the word of the Lord to me, I knew my life had been lost for a purpose. It would take many years and several more dramatic discoveries about God to find out what that purpose was.

Nothing Is Wasted

Although Paul considered his former life to be refuse in comparison to knowing Jesus Christ, on several occasions he gives thanks to God for his earlier life. Who better to lead the debates against circumcision for the Gentiles than the former Jewish zealot? Who better to develop the theology of the missionary church than the former scholar? Who better to champion Christian freedom than the former slave to the law?

Nothing is ever wasted when God converts us. What we want changed is what God wants to transform into something useful. He will use our past hurts, our long detours in the wrong direction, our old gifts and skills. He will even use all that religious stuff we've learned, and all those memory verses.

I have developed a great appreciation for the life my parents gave me as a child. I am thankful that they put me on a journey with Jesus that would continue even after they stopped being my guides. I am thankful for all the Bible stories and disciplines in the faith that they taught me. It all came back when I needed it. But most of all I am thankful that these fallible human parents dared to thirst for God. For it is not their religious traditions, their gifts, victories or failings that I have inherited, but their thirst for God. It is good to be able to tell that to my mother, whom I love so very much. I still hope that someday I will be able to tell it to Dad.

Looking Again at Born Again

We ministers get a little squeamish about telling strangers what we do for a living. I find it particularly awkward when the question emerges from the person sitting next to me on an airplane. My reply usually makes the questioner get really nervous. When the questioner finds out that I'm a Presbyterian minister, she may try to witness to me. Sometimes an evangelical Christian will say, "Yes, that's fine, but are you born again?" Well, there it is. I can either say yes and get back to work, or I can try to get at exactly what is meant by this wonderful phrase: *born again.*

Although the term is used only once in Scripture, it has become something of a catchword that signals what kind of Christian a person is. If by being born again we mean that we have joined the right group of Christians, we have made the same mistake as the Pharisees, Sadducees and Zealots, who all claimed to set the boundaries on the kingdom of God.

Jesus used the term *born again* to describe something that happens to us, something that is not a spiritual accomplishment. Being born is a rather passive process. No one ever chose to be born. No one picked a family to be born into. None of us were born because we were convinced we needed it. Jesus used the image because it describes beautifully how we enter the kingdom and find eternal life. After a lot of pain and tears, a new life is born. Whether it wants to be born is really beside the point.

My daughter's birth was very traumatic. After my wife had been in labor for thirty-six long, lonely hours, she started hemorrhaging. The fetal monitor sounded the alarm, and doctors and nurses appeared in the room immediately. I was terrified. Off she was rushed to the operating room. I went racing behind her stretcher. I arrived at the doors of the operating room to encounter a forbidding nurse. "I'm sorry," she said, "but this is quite serious. You can't come into the operating room." I couldn't think of what to say, but I really wanted to get into that room. Finally I blurted out, "But I'm a Lamaze graduate." She smiled and shut the door in my face.

The operation seemed to take an eternity. As far as I can remember, it was the only time in my life that I could not pray. I remember trying, but the fear was overwhelming. I had lost so much. Did God now want my wife and my child?

Paul wrote that the Spirit intercedes for us in prayer "with sighs too deep for words" (Romans 8:26). I know about that ministry. As I sat in the waiting room, my fear mysteriously turned to calm. I realized that I could lose everyone except my Savior. Eventually, I would have to give them all back to their Creator. Whether that happened today or not was simply up to God.

When the nurse told me everyone was fine and I was the father of a healthy redheaded daughter, I was more than relieved. I was so very thankful. My fear of losing family had become gratitude for receiving it back. When I held my daughter for the first time, that gratitude turned into an overwhelming love. I'll never forget that moment when I met her and fell in love with her at the same time. She didn't do a thing to deserve that love. Her arrival had caused great pain for my wife and even threatened her life. But she was our daughter, and we loved her.

To be born again is to discover ourselves as infants in the gracious arms of God. There is nothing we can do to make God love us more. There is nothing we can do to make him love us less. We cannot manipulate God. He won't pay more attention to us if we figure out how to become his favorite child. We assume that God's love must be tied to something—our performance, our sacrifices or at least our love for him. But Scripture is rather clear about this. God's love for us is rooted in his own merciful nature.

Becoming convinced of that grace is like—well, like being born again. We understand that even if we lost the world, the love of the Father would still be enough.

Abandoning Our Disappointments

One of the things we have to turn away from is our expectation of glory. Most of us want just a little bit of glory that will put a shine on lives that have been dulled by the harsh realities of limitations and losses. A teacher knocks herself out in hopes that she will make a real difference in one or two students every year. She would love to be recognized as the miracle worker, but she settles for an occasional thank-you note at graduation. A young employee regularly puts in overtime at the office in hopes that the CEO will walk by his desk long after everyone else has gone home. It is only a little glory, but we work very hard for it.

Usually our understanding of glory is that it comes as a momentary reward. When God brings glory into our life, though, it comes not as an achievement but as an interruption, not as a moment of recognition but as a terrifying answer to prayer.

Some of us spend most of our lives praying that God will answer a specific prayer. After a while we get so used to living without the thing we crave that the craving itself turns into our constant companion. Imagine what would happen if God actually gave us the desire of our hearts. We would have to abandon the craving that has become so much a part of life. That would be frightening.

Zechariah the priest and his wife Elizabeth had spent their whole lives praying for a child. Even after they grew old, the prayers continued. One day it fell to Zechariah to enter the holy temple and pray on behalf of the people. He had, no doubt, done this before. Year after year, like the incense he offered on the altar, Zechariah watched his prayers rise up to the skies out of sight. One day God decided to interrupt the priest's prayers.

Luke tells us that a whole multitude of people were praying

outside, as was the custom. At the same moment the priest was praying for God's intervention inside the temple. Then God sent an angel who said, " 'Do not be afraid, Zechariah, for your prayer has been heard.' . . . Zechariah said to the angel, 'How will I know that this is so?' " (Luke 1:13, 18). In spite of all the praying that is going on, when an answer comes the response is, How can it be that God has heard our prayer?

Because we have grown more accustomed to asking than to receiving, God's intervention would terrify us. We have adjusted to the harshness of life. We have learned that as long as life isn't tragic, we can tolerate the fact that it will be vaguely dissatisfying. But nowhere in Scripture does hope appear for those who have learned to cope by settling for a little glory. When Jesus was born, who were such people? Herod, Caesar, the innkeeper—they receive no angels announcing good news of great joy. God wants to give us a vision of glory, not a little happiness. In order to receive that vision, we must abandon the deals we have cut with the world—deals that leave us with a little happiness.

Actually, that is probably asking too much. It is hard to abandon even hurtful relationships or unfulfilling jobs or dissatisfying lifestyles, now that we have developed such good mechanisms for getting through each day. That is why God sometimes interrupts our prayers to help us cope by presenting us with a terrifying opportunity to receive a truly glorious mission.

It is striking how much fear the angels created when they announced the births of John the Baptist and Jesus. Zechariah, Mary, Joseph and the shepherds—they all responded in fear to the angelic announcement. That was probably the right response. Whenever God sends a messenger with good news for us, it usually means a complete abandonment of the life into which we have settled.

Conversion: A Journey from Confusion to Terror

Mary did not expect to be visited by an angel. We are told that she was perplexed by his arrival, and that she pondered the meaning of his salutation, "Greetings, favored one" (Luke 1:28). When Zechariah saw Gabriel, he was terrified because he knew this was the answer from God for which he had prayed throughout his life. But Mary wasn't a priest. She was just a young woman who was certain that if she was going to have a moment of glory in life, it would be at her coming wedding. Like most Jews in her day, Mary had also come to terms with the reality of how it is. She knew that joy is found in gathering the few good moments that happen in the ordinary routines of life. So she "pondered" the "perplexing" words she heard about God's favor.

To ponder. To be perplexed. Those are great words. They signal the beginning of a mysterious intrusion. Something is out of the ordinary. A stranger knocks on the door and delivers a cable marked urgent. The boss steps into the office, shuts the door and says, "I need to talk to you." A woman wakes up one morning feeling a little nauseated. They ponder. They get perplexed. The thin veneer of the ordinary has been scratched. They suspect that it's going to cost them plenty.

A favor from God is usually confusing. But that is just how it begins. "Do not be afraid, Mary, for you have found favor with God. And now, you will conceive in your womb and bear a son, and you will name him Jesus" (Luke 1:30-31). Then Mary says, "How can this be?" She is no longer perplexed. Now she is terrified. That is a common dynamic in conversion. Once we realize what God is up to, we move from confusion to terror.

This is how God offers a favor? A woman has one great hope for a fleeting moment of glory at her modest wedding to the carpenter down the street. She hears that she has been chosen to give birth to the Messiah. Does she immediately rejoice and say, "Yes! The other women will shun me and spread rumors about me. Joseph will probably refuse to marry me. In fact, according to the law of Moses, I could get stoned for this. But if God wants me to abandon everything I had dreamed of in order to bring hope to the world, I'll just consider myself blessed."

No, Mary didn't ask for God to grant her a favor. She had played by the rules and was still a virgin. By rights she should have been allowed to pursue ordinary dreams. But what we have coming to us by rights is exactly what God overlooks when he decides to give us his favor, his grace. And for most of us, it is very good news that we don't get what we have coming to us by rights.

Many portraits of Mary show her with a quiet, serene smile. But that is not the picture we have of her in Luke, at least not yet. At this point she has just realized that her life is out of control. How can this be? A life so well constructed has to be abandoned. A job is lost. A move has to be made. Another move. A loved one dies way too soon. These interruptions proclaim that life is not what we had hoped for. It isn't even what we had settled for. God has interrupted our ordinary expectations, as cherished as they were, to conceive something. We can't manage it. We can't even understand it. All we can do is receive it. Because if God has conceived this thing, then it is holy, and it will save our lives.

The Abandoned Community

Gabriel's response to Mary's objections was twofold. First, he assured her that it was God who conceived this. If we are convinced that it is God who has interrupted our lives, then we can keep our sanity. I have found that the human spirit can withstand almost any tragedy, if we can make sense of it or at least believe that God is in control.

41

This does not mean that every interruption in life is from God. When friends are struck by tragedy, do not tell them that it is God's will. We do not know that. But we do know that no interruption, be it tragic or delightful, is greater than our God. He can bring hope into inexplicable loss. As Joseph told his older brothers at the end of their story, "You meant it for evil, but God meant it for good" (see Exodus 50:20).

This is good news only if we give up the despairing illusion that life is only what we make of it. If we, like Mary, choose to see life as an unfolding mystery, then we realize that only God writes the final chapter.

But even that conviction was not enough. Mary also had to hear from Gabriel that she was not the only one to be interrupted by God. She had to hear about Elizabeth. She had to know she was not alone.

Elizabeth and Mary were different. Elizabeth was the wife of a big-city priest, part of the establishment. Mary was an unimportant country girl. One was too old to have children, the other was too young. In their day that meant Elizabeth was no longer a woman, while Mary was not yet a woman. But when these two found each other, their fear and dismay turned into joy and praise. It wasn't to Joseph that Mary first turned, but to another woman with whom she had nothing in common, except that they had both been abandoned by normal expectations.

To this day that is what it takes to hold the church together. It is the community of interrupted lives, where we come to confess our stories and search for God's purpose. Our congregation includes many young people. Some are new parents whose lives have been interrupted by the demands of children. Others are newly married and coping with many changes. They haven't yet found their stride as a couple. Still others are young singles who are struggling with the stress of a new job in a new town that is far from family. They all come to church, and whom do they meet but lots of older members whose lives are chronically interrupted by the relentless abandonments of aging.

If the young people listen carefully, our older members will tell them about their losses. The big house had to be sold. The lifelong career is over. Society's values have changed too quickly. Now young people seem to be running everything that these older folks worked so hard to build—the company, the country, even the church. Their kids live far away. Visits to the doctor have become very frightening.

So we gather at church, young and old alike. Some of us Mary. Some of us Elizabeth. But our common terrifying realization, that life is not what we had thought, binds us together in a unified confession that God is mysteriously at work. And in that confession, hope is conceived.

3

A Place You'd
Rather Not Go

*CONVERSION ALWAYS OCCURS EN ROUTE to places we do not
wish to go. We can get there only if we have abandoned hope
of returning to the place where we would rather be.*

The Danger of Loving Jesus

Young pastors can learn a lot from their congregations. It was
not seminary, graduate school or any of the many books I've
read that taught me the most about how to follow Jesus. It was
my parishioners. Some of them have taught me important lessons through mistakes they made. They can give dramatic tes-
timonies about how God's determination to find them was
stronger than their ability to get lost. Over the years, though,
I have learned to listen to another, more subtle, story told by
those who have not made such big mistakes, but who still find
themselves very much in need of a savior.

These lives are no less dramatic. I usually get invited into the story when a crisis has occurred, or when life has taken some unpredictable, unwanted turn. A job is lost. A lab report from the doctor brings very bad news. A child is arrested for drug possession. I listen as heartbroken Christians explain that they can't understand why this has happened. They recount their love for God, their lifelong commitment to a devotional life, the church and family. "I haven't done anything wrong!" they want to say. And yet they feel as lost and displaced as the great sinners.

It is tempting to look for some mistake they have made, so they can fix it and recover the life of their dreams. They would be grateful for my wise assistance, and I would feel good about my calling to a helping profession. However, from the times I have wandered into this temptation, I have to say that my advice has never helped. My job is to point them to their only Savior. It is impossible to do that if I try to be the savior. My tendency is to help them recover their well-ordered lives. But that may be the very thing from which they most need to be saved.

When we look at the biblical portrayal of the Savior, we discover that he has a tendency to lead us away from the places in life where we would rather be. In fact, Jesus promised that to one of his first disciples.

After the resurrection of Jesus, we are given one more conversation between Peter and Jesus (John 21:15-19). It is something like the moral to the story of John's Gospel. The conversation began after Jesus found Peter once again returning to the security of the fishing boats. It had been a confusing time to be a disciple. First Jesus was dead, and then he was risen. Then he had appeared to the disciples again, and then he was gone again. It's always tempting to return to something we count on when the Savior gets unpredictable.

But the words of Jesus became very clear one morning at a

breakfast campfire. Peter was confronted by a question from Jesus that would not go away, "Do you love me? Do you love me? Do you love me?" For three years Peter had been trying to serve Jesus. During those years he had a lot of great experiences and had learned many lessons. But his discipleship apparently boiled down to one simple question, "Do you love me?" Jesus didn't ask Peter, "What have you learned? What have you accomplished? How many converts have you made?" In the end the only question is, Do we love Jesus?

We could offer many answers to Jesus' persistent question. We could point out our responsibilities to others, how many things demand our attention or how scared we are of questions like "Do you love me?" Can't we just feed the sheep? No. When the sheep get ugly, and they will, we'll quit if we are doing it for any reason other than our love for Jesus.

We are told Peter was hurt that Jesus asked him the question three times. Maybe that was because he remembered the last time someone had asked him three questions by a campfire. Maybe it was because he had finally heard the question, and it was a hard one. All he could say was all we can say: "Lord, you know everything; you know that I love you." Indeed he knows everything, even how hesitant we are to abandon, or to be abandoned, to his love. Yet that is what he clearly desires in his disciples. It's obvious that the question "Do you love me?" is not going to go away. Jesus will keep asking it until we realize what it means to be in love with him.

After the question is raised and an answer is offered, then the mission is given. "Feed my sheep." That mission won't go away either. Jesus just keeps calling Peter to it.

I find that often people think they are called into a certain mission with life. But they aren't sure. Sometimes they are afraid that if they don't respond right away they will miss their opportunity to be of use to the kingdom. But I have not found that to be the case. If the call is truly from God, it does not go away. As Jesus was relentless with Peter, so will he constantly remind us of our mission. The more we say we love him, the more he will bring us back to our calling—feeding sheep. We feed people because they are hungry. They are hungry for meaning and purpose, for comfort and understanding. They are hungry most of all for God. After all, they are his sheep.

It seems at first like a rather straightforward mission—feed people who are hungry for God. But there is more. There is also a prediction. "When you were younger, you used to fasten your own belt and to go wherever you wished. But when you grow old, you will stretch out your hands, and someone else will fasten a belt around you and take you where you do not wish to go" (John 21:18).

To mature as a follower of Jesus means to be led to the same powerless places he was led. In the words of Henri Nouwen,

It means the road of downward mobility in the midst of an upwardly mobile world. I do not say this with sadness, but joyfully, because the downward road of God is the road on which he reveals himself to us as God with us.[1]

I heard Nouwen say those words at my seminary graduation. He was preaching on this same conversation between Jesus and Peter. It was without a doubt the most memorable sermon I have ever heard. My friends and I had just completed three rigorous years preparing to be ministers. Most of us had recently received our first parish calls, and we were prepared to venture out into the life we had been dreaming of for years. We processed down the center aisle of the great cathedral chapel at Princeton University, wearing our new pulpit gowns. We were on the brink of a great new life as pastors. We were trained, called and ready to set the kingdom of God on fire, or so we thought.

I can still see Nouwen leaning over the pulpit asking us, "Do you love Jesus? Do you love Jesus? Do you love Jesus?" He waited through a long pause. _Yes. Yes. Yes, of course I do,_ I thought, _that is why I am here._ Then he made his promise:

If you say yes, it will mean meetings, meetings, and meetings, because the world likes meetings. It means parishioners who only want one thing of you, not to rock the boat . . . it means being subjected to endless déjà vu experiences. It means all of that. But it also means anxious hearts waiting to hear a word of comfort, trembling hands eager to be touched, and broken spirits with expectations to be healed. . . . Your life is not going to be easy, and it should not be easy. It ought to be hard. It ought to be radical; it ought to be restless; it ought to lead you to places you'd rather not go.[2]

I heard that sermon a long time ago. My pulpit robe has become tattered and worn through long years of feeding Jesus' sheep. The phrase that comes back to me the most is Nouwen's promise that I would be subjected to endless déjà vu experiences, to constantly recurring episodes with a people who are always on their way but not always clear about where they are going.

Most ministers nurture a cherished self-image of being Moses, trying to lead God's people to the Promised Land. We like to think we can get them somewhere. But I am amazed at how much time we spend wandering around in the desert. I have had the same conversation about the youth group eating pizza in the church parlor at least two hundred times, in three different churches, since I have been ordained. I spend an enormous amount of my time, not holding trembling hands, but paying the rent. I am convinced that the church is different because of my presence, but I am not convinced it is any closer to the Promised Land. I am willing to risk being a failure for Jesus, and I can certainly handle success. But the one journey

I didn't want to undertake was the daily meandering of God's people. That, however, is where I am called. And I am absolutely convinced this is the only way the love of Jesus is going to make sense to my parishioners.

Nobody wants to be on the road to downward mobility. If you aspire to it, you don't understand it. It costs too much. It runs counter to the road we desire to travel—the one that leads to upward mobility. By rights, we should get to pass important mile markers that measure our success—marriage, babies, career, house, better career, bigger house. We should be on our way. So why would Jesus ask if we love him, and then, if we get the right answer, promise that we will be carried to a place we don't want to be?

What is that place? Why do we have to abandon the life we know, just to love Jesus? Maybe the answer to these questions has less to do with either the place to which we are carried or the place we leave. Maybe it has more to do with what happens to us along the way.

The Danger of Loving Jesus: Another Story

Norma was the granddaughter of missionaries and the daughter of devout parents. She was very involved in the local church she attended until she went off to a Christian college where she met the man who became her Christian husband. She had been following Jesus for a long time. She had almost attained the "happily ever after" part. Obviously the final step was for Jesus to give her a Christian family. But that was when the Savior became confusing.

She and her husband discovered they couldn't have children. After a lot of prayer and effort, they began adopting children. The first three adoptions went well. Raising babies had its moments of challenge, but Norma discovered she was a good mother. It was like Peter going back to the fishing boat when Jesus couldn't be found. The disciples of Jesus like to have another vocation to fall back on when it gets hard to follow him.

Norma and her husband had moved onto a farm. Every morning he commuted into the city to lead the large, demanding business he owned. On the farm during the day and much of the night, it was just Norma and the kids. That was about it.

During that time it seemed to Norma that the risen Lord was busy appearing to other people, but not to her. There was certainly no miracle that allowed her to give birth to her children. That disappointment, combined with a strong reaction against her rigidly conservative childhood, sent Norma into a long drift from church. The best dream she could find was to forget about the demands of Jesus and just raise kids on a farm.

Then one day a social worker called to ask if she would consider adopting Debbie, an older child who came from a troubled background. Norma was eager. This was what she knew how to do. She was sure she could change this little girl's life by filling her with love.

She was wrong.

Debbie's troubles were not about to be exorcised by good parenting and fresh air. Her early years had been ravaged by abuse, and the emotional scars ran very deep. After valiant efforts at doing everything she could, Norma realized that she didn't have what was needed to feed this hungry lost sheep who called her Mom. In her bravest moment she confessed that the problem wasn't just that she had failed in her parenting skills. The real problem was that she didn't know how to love this angry daughter. But parenting was supposed to be the one thing she was good at, the one thing for which she didn't need a savior.

She prayed for God's grace. It had already come. It was

taking her to a place she would rather not have gone.

For nine long years Norma and her husband continued on the downward road paved with disappointment, until Debbie left home. On her graduation day Debbie ran off to Chicago with her friends, skipping the graduation party Norma had planned for out-of-town relatives.

Norma had taken Debbie into her home because she thought the poor child needed to be saved. Certainly this was another opportunity to prove her ability to love, to prove her worth to God, to prove she should have been a parent because she was good at it.

Debbie was a gift from God. But she wasn't given so that Norma could prove anything. The troubled, troubling gift proved it was Norma who was the needy one, not the children she rescued. That was her moment of conversion. Now Norma knew she couldn't be the savior. Now she knew it was she who needed salvation.

After Norma was willing to accept God's unconditional love for her, it became easier to give grace to all her children without having to rescue them. When Christians really believe they need a savior, they are not as tempted to try to be the savior for others.

That happened quite a while ago. Norma and her husband have now abandoned the farm where she was abandoned by most of her ideals. They have also returned to the church. In fact, they have assumed leadership of their church's local mission programs. One of those programs offers committed relationships to youth who are identified as at risk by the local schools. When other members of the church volunteer to help out in this program, Norma spends a lot of time cautioning them about trying to fix any of these troubled kids. She tells the volunteers to expect to be rejected, and she warns them that they will not be appreciated for trying to make a difference. But making a difference is not the point. Giving love away is the point, and we can only do that if we have fallen in love with the grace of our own Savior.

Norma would have preferred easier lessons on grace. But there are no easy lessons on grace. There is just one conversion after another as we answer Jesus' question, "Do you love me?"

I continue to be impressed that Norma and her husband maintain loving relationships with all their children, including Debbie. With her parents' help, Debbie made her way through college, married and now has two children of her own. Her life is still far from perfect, but what she knows of love she says she learned from her adoptive parents.

After all these years, Norma is still learning the hardest lesson on love—how to receive it. She is still on the way. There is more conversion to come.

Betwixt and Between

It is amazing how much of our encounter of God occurs along the way in life. Abraham and Sarah had to leave their home in Ur of the Chaldees to journey toward the Promised Land. All of their spiritual growth, all the steps in their conversion, occurred along the way. At the end of his life, the only land Abraham owned was the burial plot he had purchased for Sarah. But the end of the story is not the important part. It was their long journey with God that is important.

When Moses led the Hebrew people out of slavery to that same Promised Land, the same dynamic occurred. There was a road that went directly from Egypt to Palestine called The Way of the Land of the Philistines (Exodus 13:17). But God did not lead the people that way, because he knew that if they faced war they would run back to Egypt. So he turned them south, down into the Sinai peninsula, where they would have to learn how to trust God. It was the only way slaves could be converted into a kingdom of priests.

After they had traveled about twenty miles south to Elim, the people complained because the journey was so hard. They had abandoned water and food, securities they had in Egypt. There is nothing as secure as slavery. Freedom scares us. When we are free, all we know is that we are on the way. We don't know if we will get there. We certainly don't know how we'll get there.

This journey metaphor is helpful for understanding marriage. Most pastors I know would prefer to do their premarital counseling with couples about six months after the wedding—when the newlyweds are ready to listen. By then they are about twenty miles south of where they thought they would be. They have run out of resources. They aren't sure they are heading in the right direction. They are starting to realize what their dream of marriage has actually cost. They may even begin to miss Egypt. Only in abandonment do they realize that marriage is a great journey.

Usually these couples are frightened enough to start serious conversations on what it means to have a savior for the marriage. What most of them want from me is a little advice or a book that will take care of their problems. Six months into their marriage, they want to have arrived at the Promised Land. They have so far to go, and so much mystery to discover as they are led to places they never imagined. All I can do is show them how to receive God's daily manna. It isn't much. It certainly isn't what they want. But the only way they will stay on the journey together is by learning how to receive God's daily grace for their marriage.

And that is true for all of God's people. The challenge to people of faith is to learn how to follow. Central to that task is giving up the expectation of knowing where we are going.

Jesus delivered his most severe warnings on the cost of

discipleship after he had already set his face toward Jerusalem. Much of the Gospels explains what happened to his disciples along the way to that cross. In fact, a large part of Jesus' ministry occurred on the way. Luke tells us that "as they were going along the road, someone said to him, 'I will follow you wherever you go' " (Luke 9:57). Then Jesus cautioned his disciples that abandonment awaited them. "Foxes have holes, and birds of the air have nests; but the Son of Man has nowhere to lay his head."

One of the most frustrating things about Jesus is that he just won't settle down. He is constantly moving us away from the places where we would prefer to stay, like Galilee, and moving us closer to Jerusalem, where we do not want to go.

We journey as a people betwixt and between. We journey between the security of the pseudo-life we abandoned and the uncertainty of the life waiting for us in Jerusalem. Along the way the gospel starts to change our lives. Maybe an encounter with Jesus will occur en route to a painful place like divorce, disease or a funeral. Or maybe it will begin along the way to a wedding or a birth or a great new job. We thought the road we were walking led down, or up. We thought it was the road to failure or success. But eventually we discover that it is the road toward Jerusalem, where our salvation becomes clear.

Sometimes we get to a place in life that feels so right. Our health and our jobs are good. Our family and friends are doing well. No one is leaving. It's tempting to shout, "OK. Nobody move!" Well, we had best take a picture, because the chances are great that Jesus will invite us to experience still more abandonment.

That's because Jesus will not settle for our watered-down dreams that accept life the way it is. He keeps pushing us toward a promise we cannot yet see. What is so special about Jerusalem? Most of the time the disciples don't know, except that their salvation will become clear there. In the meantime, the promise keeps them en route. That's how it changes our lives.

In the words of Margaret Farley, "The ultimate meaning . . . of the promise I make today can be clear only at the end of my life; and the meaning of my life at its end will be different because I made this promise today."[3] In making commitments we throw ourselves into a stream that flows in a certain direction. But the direction may change. The water may become rough. We won't know until the end what entering the stream today means.

Along the way Jesus will invite us to drop the things we are carrying that are heavy but deeply cherished. But don't look back. The loss is simply another step toward Jerusalem. In the Gospels Jerusalem comes at the end of the story, which means that Christian disciples spend a lot more time aware of what Jesus is leading them from than what he is leading them toward. There are such good reasons to stop. One had to bury his father. Another just wanted to say goodby. But Jesus is quite clear—the way to salvation lies ahead.

Each day on the journey, the disciple of Jesus has to make a choice about continuing. Is this the time to look back, or should we continue on? Our response to that question is how faith grows. The masters of spiritual development have known that for a long time.

In the Benedictine monasteries of medieval Europe, all of the monks wore habits of simple, unimpressive cloth as a symbol of their spiritual journey. The new novice surrendered his old clothes in exchange for the new habit. But the old clothes were not discarded. They remained in the monastery closet as a reminder to the novice that should he ever want to leave, the old clothes were waiting for him. This option forced them to choose their vocation every day.

It was for this same reason that Martin Luther claimed he had to be born again every day. Each day he had to choose to embrace his baptismal vows. Each day he had to renew his commitment to follow Jesus to places that he would rather not go.

Abandoned to a Commitment

For a long time the church has learned from the heroic commitment of men like St. Benedict and Martin Luther. It is tempting to wish we had access to these historic figures so we could learn more from them. But the church today is filled with illustrations of faith and commitment. These contemporary saints are all around us, but we cannot see them because they are wrapped in ordinary lives.

Katharine was the fourth of five children. Her younger sister Agnes, the fifth child, was born with Down syndrome. In those days doctors often recommended that such a child be institutionalized for the few years of life that it was expected to live. But Katharine's parents decided to raise Agnes at home with their other children.

With amazing patience and boundless love, Katharine's mother taught Agnes to function well around the house. She learned to cook, shop for groceries, go to church and ride the bus alone. Katharine and her other siblings treated Agnes as a vital part of their family, which in fact she was. It all seemed to be working well.

Katharine went on to graduate from high school, attend a prestigious university and embark on a demanding career with a New York City publishing house. Agnes completed the scant schooling available to her and stayed home with her parents, helping with the daily chores around the house.

Their father died unexpectedly, leaving Agnes and her mother. Three years later, the mother died. None of the children needed to discuss what would happen next. Katharine was the only one of the four older siblings who wasn't married. So she took over the care of Agnes in her parents' home. It wasn't a place she had ever expected to go. It was an interruption that occurred along the way to some other dreams.

For thirty-five years Katharine commuted from their family home in the suburbs into the city where she worked. Occasional evenings in town were scheduled to allow her to get home by Agnes's bedtime. She had to say no to any job promotions that involved travel. Dating rarely progressed beyond her response to questions about whether she lived alone.

In time, Agnes required constant supervision. Katharine works at home now, with daytime help to cope with her sister's deteriorating condition. Some nights the loneliness is overwhelming. Nobody knows how many sacrifices she has made for Agnes. But through Katharine's love and commitment, Agnes, now mentally the age of two, has just celebrated her fifty-sixth happy birthday.

Katharine is my wife's aunt. Everybody I knows addresses her as Aunt Katharine, even those whose relationship to the family is based more on hospitality than blood. She has been a surrogate mother, faithful sister and ever-available counselor to many for two generations. She is the embodiment of Christian commitment, a symbol of God's grace to our family.

Not long ago, Agnes's health declined dramatically. Caring for her has taken on Herculean dimensions. No one can predict how much longer she will live. Under their breath, some family members wonder if Agnes's death wouldn't be best for Aunt Katharine, who has given the best years of her life to Agnes. But that has never been Katharine's perspective. Life with Agnes has not been easy. Every time Agnes has a good day, Katharine considers it a victory. She hopes for more days, good or bad.

This is not the life Katharine dreamed about when she went off to college. It has bound her up and led her to a place she had not planned on going. But it is Christ Jesus who has led her there. It has become exactly the life she wants. That is what it means to be Christian.

Called to the Enemy

One of the greatest illustrations of the journey to a place we do not want to go is Jonah's call to Nineveh. It was a call he did not want to receive to a place he did not like. Nineveh was the capital of Assyria, the enemy of God's people. It was a strong city that had grown sick and decadent and needed to turn toward the grace of God. Nineveh illustrates what is wrong with the world, and what is oppressive to the church. Nineveh does not care about our Savior. It hurts us all the time.

Nineveh may be our power-driven, money-hungry workplace. It could be the violence that has overtaken our inner cities. It could be our sin-sick, self-indulgent society. Nineveh is whatever we would just as soon have God destroy. Jonah didn't want to rescue Nineveh. Neither do contemporary Christians who renounce the world more vehemently than God, who still loves the world and is not done seeking its redemption.

Immediately after the word of the Lord came to Jonah sending him to Nineveh, he "set out to flee to Tarshish" (Jonah 1:3). Tarshish lay about two thousand miles in the other direction from Nineveh.

It is striking that Jonah could not simply ignore the call of God. He couldn't stay where he was. He had to either obey the call or run "away from the presence of the LORD" (Jonah 1:3). Jonah's image of God is at stake here. He ran away because he could not accept the image he was presented. This is really not a story about the conversion of Nineveh. It's about the conversion of Jonah, which occurred as a result of his calling. As is always the case, Jonah's calling resulted from discovering a greater image of God than he had or wanted to have.

I find that parishioners who are unsure of their calling in life often begin shopping around for new jobs or schools or new cities to visit. But they never seem to pick Nineveh, unless they begin their search with a greater discovery of God. Then they are open to surprising discoveries of what his love can do in the world, and where it can lead.

We tend to use the Bible as an answer book. But the Bible is more than that. It thrusts us into an encounter with the Word of God. It is the Bible that questions us and waits for our response. When we begin with our own questions, like "Where do you want me to go?" we have to come up with our own answers. Not surprisingly, those answers always seem to be "Tarshish."

Tarshish was a far-off idealized port city, a kind of ancient Shangri-la. Solomon's fleet went there to get gold, silver, ivory and peacocks (1 Kings 10:22). Lingering around the benign peacocks of God's kingdom is more enjoyable than offering the mercy of God to the sinner, the enemy, the powerful. Every Christian I know is interested in the call of God. We all want God to call us. We just want to pick the place and the people.

As the story of Jonah and the great fish makes clear, God can find us and bring us back when we run off in the wrong direction. Do not worry about making a serious mistake and getting sidelined by God. I have heard more than one well-meaning speaker strike fear into the heart of youth with warnings that kids who make mistakes will get only God's "second best." Nowhere in the Bible do we find such a concept. We do find plenty of illustrations like Jonah, where God comes after us when we have made mistakes. We can't outrun God, we can't outwait him or outmaneuver him. We can't even outsin his mercy. The Bible is clear about this—God gets what he wants.

It can be pretty dramatic when God comes looking for us. We tend to think of grace as the concession of a polite God who says, "Well, that's all right, Sweetheart; please try not to do that again." Grace is whatever it takes for God to come and get us. It can be confrontational, frightening, disruptive and demanding, but in the end it saves our life.

Sometimes God has to come and get us when we are hiding in our grief, nurturing a broken heart. He gently whispers, "You are not alone. I love you." Sometimes he finds us lost in sin and whispers, "I forgive you and restore you." Sometimes he has to chase us down as we are heading the wrong way. That is usually when things get dramatic. It's as if God then says, "You need a savior. Let me demonstrate that to you."

The Call to Wake Up

Things got very dramatic for Jonah on board the ship bound for Tarshish. "The mariners were afraid, and each cried to his god," we are told. Interestingly, Jonah is sleeping all this time. The captain of the ship has to wake him up asking, "What are you doing sound asleep? Get up, call on your god!" (Jonah 1:5-6). Living outside the call of God is very much like falling asleep in a storm. It is as if we're missing the drama of God's activity in the world.

People don't plan on sleeping their way through life. They start out with higher expectations, maybe even a passion or two. But somehow they boarded the wrong ship. They thought it would take them to great dreams, but they were not the dreams of God. Along the way, chasing the wrong dreams, they get too beaten up, too disappointed or even too successful to take any risks. They tell themselves this is as good as life is going to get for them. With no real reason to stay awake, they just let life's voyage lull them to sleep. Maybe they work themselves to exhaustion or settle for a life that bores them into a coma. Maybe they drink a little too much at night. Just enough to pass out without having to be alone with their thoughts. Maybe they buy new toys that keep them distracted and entertained. It's all just a way of sleeping through bad choices in life.

One of the couples in my congregation decided that television was making their home life dull and lifeless. They decided they would put the TV away for three months. At the end of that time the wife announced she was pregnant. They weren't asleep anymore.

People who are living out of the calling of God have lots of highs and lows because the plans of God will take them to the heights and depths. They notice the storms that are brewing around them. They can't sleepily ignore the poor and the sick. They see the violence and oppression that tear up the lives of very real people. But they also can see signs of grace in the world if they look for them.

To respond to the call of God is to open our eyes to see God in the midst of our storm-tossed world. As Jonah had to abandon his sleepy escape and be thrown into the sea, so we too must throw ourselves into the way it really is in the world. That usually means life will be full, but it does not mean we will get crazy with busyness. People who are too busy have lost their vision for what they are doing. They fell asleep a long time ago.

The church member who gets really busy and comes to see me as pastor often wants to drop out of some volunteer project. I used to find someone else to do that person's work, no questions asked. But over the years I have noticed that the empty places I created in people's schedules always seemed to get filled up with something else equally demanding. Before long the same people are back in my office, certain that the answer to their problems in life is to simply drop another time-consuming project.

There are others in our church who work very hard on the job, raise active families, help out the PTA and maintain great commitments with some ministry or mission of the church. How do they do it? Maybe they work with their eyes open to find a vision of God in all they do. That's the secret. The goal for fatigued disciples of Christ is not to do less but to do the right things. These are the things that keep us awake to God's presence in our lives. If we find that, we can't get enough of it.

After one year in college I dropped out "to find myself." Not only had I been abandoned by the world of my childhood, I had also been abandoned by the dreams of life I once nurtured as a child. I trusted no one, least of all myself. I was the embodiment of "lost." After hitchhiking around for a while, I eventually ran out of money and wound up working the midnight shift at a gas station in New York. I wasn't in Nineveh, and I certainly wasn't in Tarshish. I had just fallen asleep somewhere along the way. I had no goals, no real relationships and absolutely no plans to be called by God.

God's wake-up call came from a homeless man named Shorty. Shorty would show up around 3:00 a.m. after a night of bumming enough money to get drunk. I would let him sleep off the alcohol in one of the rooms in the back of the station. One night as I was sitting next to the gas pumps, he staggered out to talk to me. He said, "I like you. You and I have a lot in common." That was the night I woke up.

I decided it would be better to be thrown into the chaotic, frightening sea where my future was unknown than to sleep away my life. But that meant I would have to trust people again. I would have to trust God again. I would have to abandon my cherished self-image as a victim. Doing that was like asking the sailors to throw me overboard.

After Jonah asked the sailors to throw him into the heaving sea, they tried to row him to shore. When those around us need to face their call from God, we may be tempted to save them from it—to try to reduce their problems by fixing their schedules, relationships or work. But that is futile and idolatrous. We can't be the savior. All we can do is help them step into the places where God alone can save them.

There is no safe way to Nineveh. Safety abandoned us long ago. There are many questions about the details of God's call. How will we get there? Who will take care of us? What assurances do we have that we will be successful in Nineveh? None. None. It feels like jumping overboard. When we realize that the madness of God is more sane than a life without passion, we are ready for the call.

Turning Points

God did not allow Jonah to drown. He sent a great fish to swallow him. The fish didn't rescue Jonah as much as keep him from running away. For three days Jonah had to wait in the belly of the fish, a place of powerlessness where he was very uncertain of his future. The fish was the place where Jonah's life got turned around.

The book of Jonah contains a wonderful prayer that has been preserved from that experience. In this prayer Jonah straightens out his relationship with God's calling. Typically we learn to pray best in the belly of a fish. That's because inside a great fish, either you pray or you remain scared to death.

Once the fish spits us onto dry land, we say it was the best thing that ever happened to us. The heart attack, the loss of employment, the child's drug addiction, the life-threatening disease: it may have scared us, but it also got us on the right road to life. Notice, the fish doesn't guarantee that we will get to that right place. It just holds us in a frightening place until we learn how to pray.

The Call to Just Show Up

Jonah eventually made it to "the great city" of Nineveh. When he fulfilled his calling, revival broke out. What are the odds that a reluctant Hebrew prophet is going to be successful in a huge, wicked city that is three days' walk from one end to the other? It is of concern to the preacher in me that Jonah's message is simply "Forty days and the Lord will overthrow the city." No illustrations, no felt-need grabbers, no careful exegesis of Scripture. Not even three points. Just a dire warning.

It's crazy to think that Jonah's cryptic sermon would result in a revival of the entire city. Unless the city was ready to repent. In that case, all Jonah had to do was show up.

The most important thing we do in responding to the call of God is to show up. We don't have to be certain. We don't have to be the best. We don't even have to want to be there. All that would matter if we were responsible for making changes. But we aren't. That's the life we had to abandon when we started following God's call. Now we are just responsible to show up with a vision of what God is doing in the world.

Most of the people in my congregation live undramatic lives. Their time is given to reports that have to get written, clients that have to be satisfied, mechanics who can't get the car fixed, parent-teacher conferences, laundromats and grocery stores. Most of the time they are just taking care of the mundane duties in life. Maybe it is not the life they wanted. It certainly isn't Tarshish.

While it isn't the place they had wanted to go, some of them are certain this is exactly the place to which they have been called. Actually those people don't just show up. They show up with a vision and a message about what God is doing. What distinguished Jonah in Nineveh was his vision of God's future for the city. That vision is what makes contemporary disciples of Jesus Christ the salt of the earth and the light of the world.

Our call is to live in the real world, maybe even where we don't want to live, with a world-changing vision of Christ's coming kingdom. That vision is so powerful that it can shape the future. According to Jonah 3:10 it changed the mind of God, who decided not to destroy Nineveh after all. Change the mind of God? We can do that only if somewhere along the way, maybe in the belly of a fish, we learned how to pray.

Serving a God Who Changes His Mind

It is striking that Jonah became upset when God changed his mind. He had feared that all along. In fact, that was the reason he had resisted God's call in the first place. "Is not this what I said while I was still in my own country? . . . I knew that you are a gracious God and merciful, slow to anger, and abounding in steadfast love, and ready to relent from punishing" (Jonah 4:2). Even Christians prefer the message that you get what you deserve in life. It's a harsh message, but at least we understand it, and it assures us that justice will come in the end. What we don't understand is God changing his mind. Ironically, that is what the whole story of Jesus Christ is about—God changing his mind about our sin having to have eternal consequences. We forget that part easily, however, preferring to think of God as the one who will eventually even the score with this world that has been so cruel to us. Abandoning our desire for vengeance is about as hard as it gets in following our God who is "ready to relent from punishing."

While Jonah sat outside the city waiting to see if God was really going to spare these sinners, a bush sprang up to give him shade. He was delighted. It wasn't a bush he had planted or cultivated. It was just given to him by grace. Then the bush died, and Jonah became very angry, as if he had lost that which was his by rights. God observed that Jonah felt great passion about a plant that was his only by grace only for a while, but had no passion for the 120,000 people of Nineveh.

Most of us have spent most of our life under one bush or another. It could be our health, our station in life or our family. It has shaded us from the heat of adversity. It has covered our head and made us feel secure. But we did not really earn these things. They were given to us as signs of grace. We receive them only for a while, and in the end we always have to give them back to God. Even knowing that, it would not be hard to imagine the grief we would feel if we lost any of these things. "So what about the 120,000 people of Nineveh?" God asks. "Should you not grieve their loss for eternity?"

In the narrative, God received no answer to his question. Maybe it's up to us to provide it.

4

Abandoned by Success

IT IS POSSIBLE TO GET SO LOST in the success of our choices that we assume success means our choices were right. But typically, success is just one more reason we need a savior.

Why Does Judgment Sell So Well?

After I had been in the pastorate for several years, I returned to graduate school to work on an advanced degree. It was the best thing I could have done to confirm my call to the pastorate. For a long time I had yearned for uninterrupted study. But when it came, I discovered that I missed the parish a great deal. I particularly missed the way my theology was shaped by the compromised, ambiguous lives of the people who find themselves in churches.

One day in graduate school I attended a panel discussion that was responding to the question, Why are judgmental forms of religion growing? One of the panelists was a psychologist whose thesis was that fundamentalist churches are populated by people who consider themselves exempt from the wrath of God because they are forgiven. However, she claimed, they do enjoy hearing about the judgment that is coming to the rest of the world. Next to speak was a historian of revivalism, who claimed that this type of religion is essentially an expression of social discontent that always does best when the times are hard. Faced with the loss of jobs and the loss of a future, people would almost prefer to have God blow down a little fire from the heavens and take them to a better place. Finally a sociologist and a theologian offered their considered theories as well.

Like a good student, I sat there and took careful notes, but the pastor in me wanted to stand up and scream out, "Maybe judgment sells because we think we deserve it, having been judged inadequate by our parents when we were kids and by our kids when we were parents, by our supervisors, by our lovers, and worst of all by the person who keeps showing up in the bathroom mirror no matter how many diets or self-improvement programs we try. Is it any wonder that we think God may want to judge us as well?"

I think it was for this reason that John the Baptist was such a popular preacher. Scripture tells us, "The people of Jerusalem and all Judea were going out to him, and all the region along the Jordan" (Matthew 3:5). John was a turn-or-burn kind of preacher. The crowds that gathered around John make it obvious that sermons on God's wrath were as fashionable in his day as they are in ours. Today the words these angry preachers use almost melt in the heat of their warning of an awful judgment that is to come. We flock to their churches as if we were trying to make it to the banks of the Jordan, nodding our heads saying, "Judgment? Amen. You preach it, John."

Then the strangest thing happened. Jesus the Messiah

showed up in the middle of one of John's sermons. This was the one whom John had been warning us about, the one who has the power and the right to judge us all. But to everyone's amazement, especially John's, he didn't call down fire from heaven. Instead, he stepped into the water and asked to receive this baptism for sinners.

When Jesus was baptized, his Father opened the heavens to tell those waiting for judgment that he was pleased with what had just happened. Remember how much we all longed to hear our earthly fathers say that they were pleased with us? That is what the descent of Jesus into our humanity is all about. The heavenly Father is pleased not because we have done well enough to find him, but because he has found us.

John's religion was essentially a theology of ascent. He called people to try harder, get their lives right and move up closer to God. By contrast, from the moment when Jesus stepped into those baptismal waters, it was clear that he was presenting a theology of descent. Jesus, the coming Judge, chose to descend into the ambiguities of compromised, complicated and conflicted lives.

Jesus called people to be righteous, but he despised those who had become professionals at it. He refused to condemn sinners, but he told them to sin no more. He claimed to set the prisoners free, but he was a disappointment to those who had political ambitions for him. In fact, he was such a disappointment that John eventually had to ask him whether he was the Messiah or not. The disappointments spread until eventually Jesus was killed.

We killed Jesus, not because he claimed to be the Messiah but because he became like us. That is a blasphemy against our greatest hopes for what a messiah will do. We don't want a savior who descends into our humanity. We want a savior who will rescue us from all the judgments we have faced. But haven't we learned by now that there is no hope in any scheme that promises to help us ascend out of the life we have judged inadequate? Hope, if it is going to come, has to descend.

From the day we are born, our lives are constantly measured. But we seldom measure up and can never meet our own extremely high standards, much less God's standards. The harder we try, the more lost we become. Maturity in our lives comes with the discovery that salvation is going to have to find us.

The Measured Life

One of the greatest joys of the pastorate is visiting newborn babies and their parents in the hospital. Sometimes I even get to hold the baby. I never tire of gazing at a life that is so pristine, so unaffected by the cares of the world. That is why I was a bit dismayed to learn that babies are routinely evaluated the day they are born. Most new parents in our congregation are also dismayed over these evaluations, but for different reasons.

When I went to see the Kehl baby, I found Martha quietly crying as she cradled her new daughter. When I asked what was wrong, Martha said that beautiful, brand-new Sarah Louise had a toe that turned slightly out. She had scored only a nine on the hospital's one to ten scale. Martha showed me the toe, and for the life of me I couldn't see a thing wrong with it. "I don't know what bothers me more," Martha said, "that they have this stupid test, or that my kid only made a nine." It was Sarah's first day of life, and she was already having trouble scoring high enough.

Martha took this test very seriously, but she also took her faith seriously. I offered as many platitudes as I could about her beautiful baby, but it didn't help very much. Then Martha asked me if I thought Communion could be received through the womb. I had to admit it was a new question for me (while thinking to myself that it would make a great question for ordination exams). She said she'd received Communion the previous Sunday in church and took some comfort in believing that the symbols of Christ's body and blood had made their way to baby Sarah Louise, even before she was born. That's important, she said, because little Sarah would need all the signs of grace she could get before the measuring took over.

Life is a gift. If we really believe that, trying to earn a life would seem ridiculous. Jesus said, "Those who save their life will lose it." To try to save our life destines us to constant measurements. Have I done enough? Have I tried hard enough? How do I compare with those around me? Am I leaving a great enough legacy for those who will remember me after I am gone? It's relentless. In fact, there is no better way to lose your life than to constantly measure it.

Our society can't evaluate its health apart from measurements. Daily our papers offer us another index on the economy, employment or some leader's popularity, as if these were good indicators of the quality of our life together. But we have yet to develop a measurement for any of the things that were important to Jesus, like loving God with all our heart and soul and mind and strength and loving our neighbors as ourselves (Mark 12:28-34). I would love to pick up a newspaper one morning that reported the percentage of Americans who have turned the other cheek, loved their enemies, fed the hungry, given a cup of water to the thirsty, welcomed the stranger, clothed the naked, cared for the sick and visited those in prison (Matthew 5:38-48; 25:31-46). But that is not likely to happen, because our system of measurement is based on values quite foreign to the kingdom of Jesus Christ.

At funerals the economic measures of success almost never make it into the eulogies. I have yet to hear a family member stand before the congregation and recount the number of dollars earned by the deceased. They want us to think that this person was loving and kind, even if he wasn't. This sentiment illustrates that in our hearts we know, we just know, that in light of eternity we have spent our lives being measured by the wrong standards. So why does it bother us so much when God is gracious enough to save us from the world's success?

Jesus Was a Lousy Salesman

It is a great challenge for preachers to present the teachings of Jesus to congregations that live in a success-driven world. My congregation has been told all week, in a hundred ways, that they are essentially consumers. Their worth, they hear, is directly related to their buying power, and their buying power is related to how hard they work. As consumers they have rights to good service and quality and the best price possible because they worked hard to earn their money. Then on Sunday they run into Jesus, who refuses to offer discounts and deals or let them have it their way. Instead he warns them about the excessive cost of being his disciple. "Whoever comes to me and does not hate father and mother, wife and children, brothers and sisters, yes, and even life itself, cannot be my disciple" (Luke 14:26).

What does Jesus mean when he says that the first will be last? The meek usually inherit nothing, certainly not the earth. If somebody takes my coat, I'm just thankful that the thief didn't get the cloak too, and I'm usually not going to offer it. Imagine applying for a mortgage and telling the loan officer, "I don't store up treasures on earth or worry about tomorrow, for tomorrow will bring worries of its own" (Matthew 6:19, 34).

As a preacher, I am tempted to find some way to water down Jesus' words in order to sell them to the congregation, as if I too believed they were consumers. *They don't know what to do with this,* I tell myself. *They're coming here to find some-*

thing that will help them get through the week. If I don't give that to them, they'll go somewhere else. About then I know that I have to spend a lot more time in prayer before I return to writing the sermon. My own drive to be a successful preacher has caused me to understand the members of the body of Christ as shoppers and myself as just one more advice peddler. In prayer I confess and get the relationships straightened out. I don't have to market God as the scratch for the itch of the day. The late theologian H. Richard Niebuhr claimed that the church is never more worldly than when "it thinks of itself as responsible to society for God rather than to God for society."[1]

My calling is terrifying but actually quite simple. I'm supposed to deliver the word of God, not rescue it. Of course, Jesus' words are scandalous to those who are used to saving their lives. But if preachers keep offering Christian principles for becoming more effective and successful in a world that is heading in the wrong direction, we will simply help our people run faster from God.

Some churches have recognized this danger and call their people to work harder at living by these hard teachings of Jesus. The preachers of these congregations take on the appearance of John the Baptist, regularly calling the real Christians to avoid the world that is quite literally going to hell. They set up standards of conduct and belief that are the norms of a holy people and encourage their people to work harder and become more successful in leading distinctive, holy lives. Ironically, these preachers are the greatest accommodationists to the world that insists we can save ourselves if we just work a little harder. Christianity isn't something we get good at. If the goal is to receive the love of God, then the only way to progress in the faith is to confess how lost we have become.

Jesus' teachings are not hard; they are impossible. Those who first heard Jesus' statement that the rich man is like a camel trying to pass through the eye of a needle were shocked. They asked, "Then who can be saved?" The Savior's response was that while it is impossible to be a Christian, all things are possible with God. It always, always gets back to receiving grace. But if we are used to earning our own way, nothing could be harder.

Betting Your Life

In the economy of God, failure is not the opposite of success. It is breaking even with life. Failure is refusing to risk what will happen if we follow Jesus. Scripture is loaded with illustrations of people who made tremendous mistakes with their lives, but God could always redeem those mistakes for good. Abraham, Moses, David, Elijah, Peter and Paul all had what by the world's standards are moments of great failure. But these are the Bible's greatest examples of people of faith. Those who are condemned in the Bible were too afraid to fail. These include the Hebrews who refused to enter the Promised Land because their spies told them about the giants in the land, the rich young ruler who could not give up his wealth and the servant who buried his talent in the ground so he wouldn't lose it. God can turn our mistakes into his victories, but he will not save those who do not trust his salvation. That is asking a lot. It is asking us to bet our lives on God's nature to be graceful. And we know God's grace often shows up after the cross.

The greatest illustrations of faith in the Bible are not provided by patriarchs and apostles, but by a couple of poor widows. The widow from Zarephath (1 Kings 17) was a particularly pathetic figure who was just barely surviving the drought with her son when Elijah found her. The prophet promised her that if she used her last bit of meal and oil to cook him a meal, her supplies would not run out until the drought was over. She did as he asked, realizing she had just bet her life that God's prophet was trustworthy.

When Jesus watches the widow put her last two coins in the temple offering, we almost want him to tell her to keep her offering. Certainly she needs it more than the temple. But Jesus says, "Truly I tell you, this poor widow has put in more than all those who are contributing to the treasury. For all of them have contributed out of their abundance; but she out of her poverty has put in everything she had, all she had to live on" (Mark 12:41-44). She has bet her life that God will take care of her.

Who are these women of faith? We don't even know their names. They are just ordinary, anonymous figures who appear in Scripture only long enough to do something wonderful. Their faces are hidden in the shadows of the story. All we can see is their need and the incredible choices they made.

When we come before God, our situation is as desperate as those of these impoverished, nameless widows. When Jesus scoffed at the wealthy, it was because they were betting on their money. Most of us don't consider ourselves to be wealthy, but we are certainly counting on something to get us by just in case God doesn't pull through. We are busy collecting whatever currency we value: relationships, achievements, money, health, being the pretty child or being the smart one—pennies to which we cling for our salvation. But no matter how many pennies we collect, we can't save our lives.

When we are abandoned by the things we value, when we discover that no matter how much we have gathered we do not have enough, when we realize that even in the currency we value we are very poor, we are ready to start talking to God. Not before. Faith means betting our lives on the grace of God.

We are told that Elijah's promise was fulfilled, and the widow at Zarephath did not starve as she had expected. But we are not told what happened to the woman Jesus found in the temple. We want to believe that things went well for her, but we are not told that. That's typical of the New Testament. It confronts us with a promise from antiquity and a risk for today. That is what makes room for our faith. We don't have trouble believing God can provide or that he took care of those poor women. But will he take care of us?

It is important not to provide reassuring answers to that question too quickly. Our faith is in the character and love of God. But he is not on a leash. He is not even predictable. The promise of the Bible is that he will indeed save our lives, but that may cost us everything that we hold dear.

The Job Syndrome: Is God Arbitrary?

I have always found the book of Job troubling. I am certainly impressed with Job, but it is the book's portrayal of God that is so unsettling. Job was a righteous man who was "blameless and upright, one who feared God and turned away from evil" (Job 1:1). One day, apparently to prove a point to Satan, God allowed everything to be taken away from Job. Even after losing his property, wealth, children and health, Job refuses to curse God. But he does not understand God's arbitrary actions. Neither do I. Why was this righteous man abandoned by everything he valued? What possible lesson could be worth such a great price?

Job is not the only passage in the Bible where God appears arbitrary. In Acts 12 we are told that Peter and James were arrested at about the same time. Peter was rescued from prison by an angel, but the Savior allowed Herod to kill James. No explanation is given. Why was Abel's sacrifice acceptable to God when Cain's was not? Why did God harden Pharaoh's heart instead of softening it? Why did Jesus choose those particular men to be disciples? Why was Lazarus raised from the dead but not John the Baptist? It was Jesus himself who reminded us that God makes the sun to shine upon both the evil and the good and sends rain upon both the righteous and the unrighteous (Matthew 5:45). We would like God to be a bit more rational.

The reader suffers through thirty-seven chapters of Job's laments and his friends' unhelpful insights, before finding something like a reason why he suffered. And the reason given does not answer why as much as who—who laid the foundations of the earth and who is the creature without understanding. In other words, when abandonment comes, we can ask, Why? But the answer we will probably get is, Who? Amazingly, that response seemed to answer Job's anxieties. The story began with Job asking why his confusing God was so arbitrary, and it ends with his new appreciation for God's mystery.

Maybe I find Job's story troubling because I keep running into it in the congregation I serve. We have no shortage of righteous people who are experiencing serious abandonments, and no one can explain why. Doug is a good example, not because his story is particularly dramatic, but because it is illustrative of the abandonments of success that are quite common.

Doug was raised in a Christian home. His father was a highly respected Christian businessman and pillar of the church. Shortly after Doug graduated from college, he went to work for his father's construction firm. The father had always affirmed Doug for being a hard worker, and he was happy to know that one day the business would be run by his son.

The father had started the company as a small local business, but Doug could see tremendous potential for expansion. For many years the two worked together, and the business gradually grew and prospered. Eventually the father grew old and turned the business over to Doug, with a warning not to lose it. Doug loved his father a great deal and was eager to demonstrate that the father's trust was well placed in his hands.

Under Doug's capable leadership the business continued to grow and expand. By the time his father died, the company was a multimillion-dollar venture that was constructing skyscrapers in several large cities. Doug had to buy his own company plane and hire pilots just to keep up with appointments. Although he worked hard to build the company, Doug was the first to say that God had blessed it. In a strange sense, that acknowledgment increased pressure on Doug to succeed as a good steward of these blessings from God.

Concerned that he was not as successful in personal devotional life as he was in business, Doug committed himself to a better prayer life. It had been a goal of his since childhood to have a time of daily prayer. At the age of forty-nine that finally became a reality for him. He wasn't sure why this devotional time was working, but he accepted it as a gift from God as well. He joined a small weekly prayer group with some other Christian businessmen. This was the life he had wanted since he was a young boy. He was a successful Christian businessman.

In his prayers, Doug began to pray that his life would take a new direction. He wasn't sure what that meant, but he had discovered that God's blessings were good, and he wanted to be open to the next gifts God might bring into his life. His prayers were answered. It was time for Doug to discover more about his God than he wanted to know.

Not long after Doug began these prayers, a change in the tax laws sent his heavily extended construction business into serious trouble. That was the same year his cherished vacation home in Canada burned to the ground. That was also the year Doug discovered that his oldest son was a drug addict.

The business slipped away day by day. Part of the agony was witnessing the inevitable slide. He tried everything, but there was no reversing the demise of his business. After years of hard struggle and exhausting legal battles, after years of selling off the business bit by bit, one day it was gone. The company plane, the big office building and the big house next door to the governor's mansion were all sold.

During this time, Doug also attended family therapy and Al-Anon for his son's addiction. They taught him a great deal about the limits of his hard work. He couldn't fix his business, and he couldn't fix his son. But what troubled him the most was that he couldn't fix his God and make him rational. Why was all of this happening? It seemed so arbitrary.

After a great deal of heartache and treatment, Doug's son pulled out of his drug addiction. But Doug was as mystified by his son's recovery as he had been by his addiction. Other people don't survive drugs. Why had his son made it? Did God decide to save him? Why? During this time the wife of one of the men in his prayer group developed cancer and died very quickly. It didn't make sense why such a wonderful woman should die and others he knew were surviving with the same disease. Then there was the difficulty of accounting for the failure of his business. He had been over it a thousand times in his mind. Maybe he had tried too hard. Maybe he had let the company get ahead of itself. But nothing he could think of could justify why all his hard work had failed him.

Doug's success began to abandon him eight years ago. During those years he has continued to rise early every morning to read the Bible, pray and sometimes wrestle with his God. He has never received a clear answer as to why he lost the business, but these days that is less important to him. He has learned to value his relationship with God that has grown so deeply since he has been talking so much to him. If forced to explain God's ways, he would still have to say they seem arbitrary. But he would add a reminder that God's mysteries have always drawn him closer to his Savior. It seems that the difference between an arbitrary God and a mysterious one lies in the eye of the beholder.

At the end of Job's story his fortunes were restored twofold. We have not reached the end of Doug's story, but it doesn't look as if that is going to happen to him. Doug is losing interest in being a big deal. He has turned into the conversion that God offered him.

When a local magazine publishes an annual list of the community's most influential businesspeople, Doug's name is no longer on it. There was a day when the editor of that magazine couldn't even get an appointment with him. Now Doug and the small property management business he runs are considered uninfluential by all his former peers who continue to be successful. He admits that still hurts, but when he adds up the lost and found columns in his life he knows he has received things of far greater value than what he lost. He lost his business, a lot of money, the respect of some peers and the hope of turning the business over to his sons, as his father did for him. He lost his former image of a God who blessed his faithful servants with success and rescued them from pain. But he also lost the need to work harder to prove his worth to both his father and his God.

What Doug has found is a new vocation—a calling to love our God, who saves us from all the things we do to make us worthy of a love that can only be received. Having discovered this amazing love, Doug now finds it easier to offer it to those around him. His relationships with his wife and all his children, including the one who needed some tough love along the way, have grown far deeper than in the days when Doug's only successes were outside the home. One of his great joys was to discover that God still had a use for all those years in the construction industry. Doug was instrumental in launching a desperately needed community development corporation with an African-American church in town, and he continues to give it a great deal of time, which he now has to give. The conversion God creates in our life always manifests itself in a passion for Christ's mission in the world around us, and nothing is ever wasted.

Recently Doug told me he now believes that when Jesus takes us to a place we would rather not go, it really is a better place. But realizing the truth of that is a gift we don't receive until later, when we look back and remember who we were compared to who we are now—or more important, who we thought God was compared to the mysterious God we now know as Savior.

The Freedom of Having a Mysterious God

Since the days of the exodus, one of the hardest things for God's people to accept is that they have a God whose ways are not their ways. For this reason the Hebrews were once tempted to have a god of wood and stone that would be predictable and familiar. People today turn to the gods of power and wealth for the same reason, because we understand these idols. The best thing, we think, about these gods is that they expect us to work hard to contribute to our own salvation. But of course that means they are not gods at all, for a true god cannot be dependent on the labor of its creatures.

When Yahweh gave his name to the Hebrews on Mount Sinai, he said to them, "I am the LORD your God, who brought you out of the land of Egypt" (Exodus 20:2). In the Hebrew culture to reveal a name was to describe the character of someone. God's name means deliverer. Thus to take the name of the Lord in vain is not to allow him to be the God of our salvation.

Any time we think we can find salvation in our hard work,

we are in grave danger. If our hard work fails or (worse yet) if it succeeds, we are stuck with ourselves for a god. That means we have destined ourselves to journeying through life's wilderness assuming that the solution to every problem is to try harder.

People who live without a mysterious Savior that they cannot always understand, much less control, live without any sense of awe or wonder to their lives. Nothing amazes or astonishes or overwhelms them, because their world is too small for God to fit into it. That is an awfully sad world that unfortunately has become quite crowded today. But I have discovered over and over again that God loves us too much to abandon us to that. He will come looking for us as he did for the Hebrews in slavery. And when he finds us, he will free us from anything that has kept us in bondage—especially our success.

5
Abandoned by Health

GOD DID NOT BECOME HUMAN THAT WE might become gods, but that we might become more fully human. Not only is brokenness an essential characteristic of being human, it is also our best opportunity to live with a Savior. Thus the healing that Jesus offers has little to do with our dreams for getting better.

Diseases That Give Us Life

John sat down at his desk and stared at the phone. He knew he had to make the call, but he just couldn't seem to do it. Finally he picked up the receiver and dialed the numbers but hung up quickly before he heard a ring. He buried his face in his hands as the tears welled up in his eyes.

John is a distinguished, middle-aged professor of philosophy at a prestigious university. He has cancer. It has metastasized throughout his body. The call he was trying to make was to his grown children. He had been able to tell his wife and his closest friends without breaking down. In fact, he had even tried to console them. But the severity of his condition finally hit home when he tried to tell his children that their father was going to die.

It is tempting to think that we are our children's god. We assume responsibility for their birth. We give them names, nurture them with love, provide for them, set the rules for their conduct and explain the world to them. All this sounds like the function of a god. That is why no one can hurt us quite like our children after they discover our feet of clay.

Inevitably every child realizes that the parent does not have all the answers to all the questions, or that the family has some problems, or that there are things about the parent that are "just so embarrassing." Those are the flaws we expect our children to find as they become individuals. But even after they leave home and start their own families, we can still maintain some watered-down approximation of the myth that we are more than human in the eyes of our children. Telling a child you are going to die, however, will rip the myth apart.

John wasn't just struggling with how to break the bad news to his kids. With that phone call he was admitting to himself that he was at best a human, who was going to die (as all humans must) because he had a disease he could not make go away.

John became a philosophy professor because he believed that teaching people to think rationally would bring about a saner world. Developing cancer is painfully ironic to him because it is such an insane disease. It makes no sense for the body to turn on itself as some cells arbitrarily destroy others. There is no satisfying philosophical explanation for cancer.

John had worked hard to distinguish himself professionally, thinking that if he was profound in his teaching and writing he would surely earn a place in the hearts of those he admired. After the news of his cancer became public, he discovered that no one really wanted to talk about how influential his work had been. Instead they all wanted to talk about how influential *he* had been in their lives. John still can't quite believe that all along it was the person and not the work that earned the respect of those around him.

After learning that he was seriously ill, John made a list of all the things he wanted to do, the places he wanted to go and the people he wanted to see before he died. For the next two years he traveled as much as he could, and he talked to everybody he loved. It was a good experience. It was, in fact, the best experience of his life. The only sad part was the constant realization that he could have been doing this during the fifty years before he got sick.

John is one of many church members who have cancer. They are a special circle of people who are all discovering that their lives are not progressing as they had planned. And yet every member of that circle would affirm that it was not until perfect health had abandoned them that they discovered how to value this marvelous gift called life.

People who have cancer are never romantic about it. They frequently feel very sick, more often from the treatment than from the disease. They are not glad they have cancer, and they do not wish it on anyone else. But if they have admitted that they have this terrible disease and that it isn't going to go away easily, then their perspectives on life are always changed. Each day is received as the gift that it is. Nobody lives for tomorrow. Relationships never take a back seat to work. Work is pursued, if possible, not to be productive but for the sheer joy of the work. And it is very important to people with cancer that they tell the people they love how they feel.

Typically, one of their great frustrations is that it took cancer to make these changes in their lives. Their other frustration is that they can't convince their healthy, hardworking loved ones that being productive is not a good way to spend a life.

Praying for Healing

Every Sunday morning after worship our pastors and elders meet in the chapel to pray with those who need healing in their lives. Occasionally we offer an evening worship service that features biblical teaching about healing and prayers for those in need. Those evening services are quite a scene. There are three kneelers at the front of the chapel. Standing behind them are three pastors and three elders. In front of us are long lines of people who are waiting for prayer. It is the great procession of the broken body of Christ. Many are there with broken health. Others have come for prayer over other broken things like marriage vows or hearts that have almost torn in two from grief.

We always make it clear that the only healer is Jesus Christ and that the pastors and elders are there not to perform magic, but to pray and hold people before their Savior. But still they come. We hear it all at those kneelers: AIDS, depression, bankruptcy, hearts that don't work, children in trouble and guilt, so much guilt. The amazing thing is that most of these people look so good on the outside. But inside they are sick and yearning for a savior.

Often we pray and pray for the sick, only to watch their health get worse. The first time I conducted one of those services, a woman walked down the aisle and asked me to pray about her crippling arthritis. I prayed my heart out for her that night. Later that year she came down the aisle using a cane. Again she knelt before God, and again I prayed and prayed that God would heal her from this crippling disease. About six months later she came down the aisle in a wheelchair. This time the elder and I kneeled before her asking God to be merciful. When I finished, she had the brightest smile on her face and said, "He is merciful, Pastor. Thank God he has healed my heart that used to be so crippled with anger. At long last I am a free woman." And again, the pastor learned something about grace from the abandonments of his parishioners. It was never her body that she was worried about. It was her heart all along. It was not until her body stopped working that her heart began to work.

If we told the truth, every one of us would have to admit that we belong in that line of broken people who come to the church looking for healing and hope and salvation and reasons to keep going another week. And by the grace of God we are finding it all. It always, always comes. Not as we had hoped or expected, because we never hope big enough. When the healing of God comes, it goes to the deep hurts, the ones we often didn't even know we had.

Do You Want to Be Healed?

Historians tell of a legend about the pool at Bethesda. According to this legend, an angel of the Lord occasionally went down into the pool and stirred up the water. Whoever stepped into the pool first, after the waters were blessed, would be healed of whatever disease he or she had. It was a commonly held belief. It even made it into some of the ancient copies we have of John's Gospel.

One day as Jesus was passing by the pool, he noticed an invalid who had waited by this pool for thirty-eight years (John 5:2-15). He kept trying to be first into the waters, but because there was no one to help him, he never made it. Thirty-eight years of trying. Thirty-eight years committed to the same plan for healing.

Simply because we are human, all of us deal with brokenness. Some of us deal with broken bodies, others with broken relationships, broken hearts, broken dreams or broken spirits. Most of us are getting by despite these problems. We tell ourselves it is not that big a deal. We've learned to compensate and to distract ourselves with busyness. But in our most honest, bravest moments, every one of us would admit that it would be good, just once, to be the first one into the pool. We would love to have an angel fix whatever is broken.

However obvious or subtle our brokenness may be, most of us deal with it the same way this invalid did. We've heard tales about what we need to do, and we have our plan for getting better. Maybe we are not still on plan A. But most of us have something going that we are certain will make everything OK, take away the hurt and give us hope.

Some us have given up on plans for ourselves and have chosen now to deal with the personal hurts by coming up with plans for our kids. God help them. When our daughter was about five, we eagerly anticipated her first ballet recital. She was one of fifty darling but not particularly gifted little dancers. At the conclusion of an "interesting" performance, I overheard one father say to his wife, "Well, there is always ROTC."

If one plan doesn't work, just try another. Work harder, try a new relationship, a new move, a second career. Maybe it is time to go back to school. There are lots of plans for getting into the healing waters. They will surely pay off, any day now. But the great danger of our plans is that they blind us to the presence of God. When Jesus the healer passes by, we may not recognize him as our Savior. "When Jesus saw him lying there and knew that he had been there a long time, he said to him, 'Do you want to be made well?' " (John 5:6). Why would Jesus ask that? Of course the man wants to be healed. He has been trying for years. But there is a difference between being worried about brokenness and wanting to be well.

After a while we can get so used to the pain that it comes to be the most reliable companion in our lives. After a while we can find so much meaning in suffering that to be made well would confuse us. C. S. Lewis described this as a clawed lizard that we wear on our shoulders.[1] It hurts us all the time. It whispers the most awful things into our ears. But we cannot let God take it away. Because the lying lizard has become our pet, the only thing we count on. So Jesus' question persists, "Do you want to be healed? Do you *really* want to be healed?"

"The sick man answered Jesus, 'Sir, I have no one to put me into the pool when the water is stirred up; and while I am making my way, someone else steps down ahead of me' " (John 5:7). We just know that if Jesus didn't interrupt him, the man was about to suggest that Jesus form a committee to devise a more equitable numbering system to ensure that he would get a turn.

But "Jesus said to him, 'Stand up, take your mat and walk.' At once the man was made well, and he took up his mat and began to walk" (John 5:8-9). Notice that Jesus didn't help the man with his plan to get into the pool. He didn't get him married or divorced. He didn't get him a new job that paid better. He didn't set him up with friends. He didn't do anything that would distract the man from his brokenness. What Jesus did was heal.

Those of us who have bodies that hurt need to remember that Jesus' healing does not necessarily mean a return to physical health. We have been invited to pray for that, but it is not promised. There is a big difference between physical health and healing. I have buried a lot of parishioners who suffered from awful diseases but died healed from their hurts.

The Bible promises that Jesus will heal the sickness in our souls. He heals the deep hurts that ache over what we have done and left undone, over the expectations of life that have not come true, over the brokenness in our families. Jesus is the Savior who encounters us in the midst of our futile plans for making life better. He calls us to see that he is with us. Salvation is now his business. So we can get up and receive the gift of life, no matter how broken it may appear.

According to John 5, no one has a harder time with healing than religious people. Confronted with God in the form of Jesus, the Pharisees kept saying, "We know about God. We know how salvation works. This isn't it. It is the sabbath. You can't heal today." Apparently even the religious have plans. The Pharisees' plan was committed to the law, and because of it they missed the miracle. Christians also have plans. We have plans for the world and the church. We have plans for others and plans for ourselves. These plans aren't bad or wrong, but they are powerless to heal. Only God can heal.

Finally Jesus told the man, "Do not sin any more, so that nothing worse happens to you" (John 5:14). That's a fascinating thing to say. In chapter 9 of John's Gospel, we are specifically told sickness is not caused by sin. So the man's sin had nothing to do with his paralysis. His sin was that he didn't recognize his hope when Jesus appeared.

The Bible is always hard on those who do not recognize their Savior. The Healer is with us, and he is with this world that is running out of plans. The only questions are: Can we see him? Can we hear him calling out to us? Get up. Take your mat and walk. Walk away from hurt. Walk as one who walks with a Savior.

When the Pastor Gets Sick

One Sunday morning as I was shaving, I noticed a lump on my throat. Later that day in church I ran into one of our elders who is an ears, nose and throat doctor. I apologized for bothering him with this but asked him if the lump was something I should worry about. He took a quick look and said he wanted to see me in his office the next morning. The early-morning appointment turned into a full day of tests. Finally the doctor told me that the lump was a tumor growing out of my thyroid gland. He was almost certain it was benign but would have to remove it to make sure.

I was also certain that it was benign, because I had just accepted a call from the National Presbyterian Church in Washington, D.C., to become their new senior pastor. The interviewing process had been very long and very thorough, but both I and the search committee had become confident that God had brought us together. So I asked myself why he would lead me into this new ministry only to let me have cancer. It didn't make sense. The tumor could not possibly be malignant.

But it was.

Three surgeries later, the doctors were optimistic about getting all the cancer, but my thyroid gland and a few other things were now missing from my neck. I had never thought of myself as being particularly gifted, but I had always cherished my capacity for hard work. I never admitted it, but I have long assumed that I got every academic degree, every job, maybe even every relationship in my life as a result of trying really hard. It is the ultimate offense against God's grace. It is idolatry, and God was about to save me from it. I was ready to step into the greatest professional challenge of my life. All I was missing was my thyroid—the gland that regulates energy.

I cautioned the elders of the church in Washington about the cancer, but they said they were still sure that God had called me to come. After a number of months, when the correct dosage of thyroid replacement medicine had been calculated, I was hard at work in my new ministry. I was determined to make sure none of my parishioners would think they had called a lemon to be their pastor. Often I would get to the church by 7 a.m. and stay until 10:30 p.m., when the security guard came around to turn on the alarm. It was as if that experience with cancer was just a meaningless fluke. Then came time for my six-month checkup. I was sure it would verify my assumption that the cancer was gone. Again I was wrong. The cancer had metastasized into my chest.

Washington is filled with self-important people who are struggling to acquire power. And this power is not limited to aristocrats. According to our local myths, anyone can come to D.C., work hard and hustle into being a somebody. I moved here equipped with the perfect neurosis for this town. Unless, of course, I really wanted to be a minister of God's grace.

Once the doctors found the metastasis, everything changed for me. For the first time in my life it occurred to me that I would not live forever. In fact, I had a disease that could take away my life.

I had to check into another hospital for more radiation therapy. This time the dosage was so high that I was not allowed to have any visitors. The nurses left my food at the door and hurried out as if I had leprosy. I was alone with my thoughts. It was as if God was giving me a second chance to get the message: This time I want you to think about it.

I had frequently visited cancer patients in the hospital. For many years I had even led a weekly support group for them. Still, it had never occurred to me that I could get this awful disease. Not when I had so much to do. Not when God needed me. But alone with my Bible and my prayers, it became so clear. God does not need me. I need him. I need him, even to be alive today. And I am grateful every day when he gives me that gift.

So I know about healing. The radiation has worked well, and I hope the cancer is gone for good. But I know that it can return anytime. Still, I am confident that I have been healed, converted, from a life that pretends it does not need grace. That could only have happened after I abandoned my certainty about tomorrow.

Abandoning Certainty

Nancy had fought her leukemia for a long time. There were days when she thought she was gaining on it, and there were other days when the awful disease seemed to be winning the battle. But all of her uncertainty came to an abrupt end when she mistakenly received a copy of her doctor's letter to another physician. It stated that Nancy had less than six months to live.

She was dazed by this discovery. She told no one. She hadn't really even told herself. It hit her one afternoon while she was shopping for groceries. As she went down one of the store aisles, she remembered that she needed a box of baking soda. After finding it on the shelf, she absent-mindedly checked the expiration date that was stamped on the top of the box. Then it caught up with her. As she later said, "I just stood there crying the angriest tears. This stupid box of baking soda was going to outlive me. I wanted a later expiration date."

Nancy was fond of telling that story a year after her six months were up. On the day that the box of baking soda expired, several of her friends threw an "I'm Still Alive" party for her. The highlight of the event was a ceremonial burying of the baking soda that she had outlived. She continued to enjoy her life one day at a time because she had abandoned all illusions about knowing how long she would live.

As long as she thought she only had six months left, each day was one day closer to the end. Six months quickly became five and then four and three and two. Finally she thought she had only a month left. She tortured herself with the question *What do I do with just a month?* She was too sick to do anything dramatic and too discouraged to do anything hopeful.

But during the days that followed those six months, after she discovered that life is too mysterious to predict, she was able to live in the hands of her Creator, grateful for each day that was not promised to her.

One day Nancy went to the hospital for another blood transfusion and did not come home as quickly as she had in the past. When I visited her in the hospital, it seemed clear that she was going to die. We talked a long time about this wonderful gift called life, and how humbling it is just to receive it without controlling it. We talked about the equally mysterious aspects of eternal life. Nancy said she wasn't too worried about that. During her days on earth she had learned a lot about receiving life as a grace. Now she was ready to receive grace for eternity.

None of us know when the end of life will come. Only when we abandon all illusions that count on tomorrow will we ever have life, which can only be received with gratitude as God's gift today.

The Bounty of God's Grace

Healing creates a thirst to express gratitude and love toward God. Every time I pray for someone to be healed, I get more and more thankful. That is not because I know God will make the sick healthy. It is just so good to know that I and these broken parishioners I love so much are all in the hands of our God. Those are such good and caring hands. I know he will heal. He may not make us healthy, but I know he will heal the sick soul and the despairing heart. It is such an amazing grace to be placed in God's hands, that if we really knew the value of it, we would not be so anxious about getting better.

Most Christians seem to have certain passages of Scripture that hound them most of their lives. For me, one such passage comes from the words of the psalmist who asks, "What shall I render to the LORD for all his bounty to me?" (Psalm 116:12).

I keep thinking about all the Lord's grace that I have received. All of the people God brought into my life when I was about to slip through the cracks. My family, my church, my health, so many incredible friends, the new day—there were no guarantees that I would have any of that. They certainly did not come to me because I deserved them. They have come only as the bounty of God's grace.

Like everyone who goes through life with open eyes, I am painfully aware of the many abandonments I have experienced along the way. In all honesty, I am not particularly thankful for those painful losses. Those who suffer through the loss of their health are not happy about their broken body, any more than widows are happy about the loss of their husbands or bankrupt businesspeople are happy about the loss of their success. The reason people who have lost their lives are grateful is that they have been found by their Savior. He has given them a new life. It may not look all that different from the life they had before, but for them, everything is different. Even the morning sunrise is received as a precious gift that can overwhelm them with thankfulness.

Gratitude may be the ultimate vocation for the Christian. We engage in whatever mission the Lord has given us not because we must, but because we may. People who are thankful for all the grace they have received want more than anything to give gifts. But we have to lose a great deal of life before we discover that the purpose of life is to give it away to things that matter.

If we are grateful, we cannot help but live our lives as a witness to God's salvation. If we are not grateful, no matter how hard we try, we can never have a Christian vocation. That's because Christians discover their mission only as a response to being in love with the grace of God.

The front cover of our church bulletin claims that our congregation is "a ministry of grace, passionate about Christ's mission in the world." We can know what we are supposed to do only when we have had a real encounter with our merciful God. Once we have received grace, we inevitably get passionate about helping the world to receive it. The more we try to engage in that mission, however, the more we realize how dependent we are on God. If Christians try to make a difference in the world relying only on their zeal (or worse yet on their guilt), they will inevitably fail. But once they have become good at recognizing the Savior when he appears, they realize that their mission is not to change the world. Their mission is to teach the world to see the grace of God. People who have been touched by the healing hands of Jesus Christ tend to recognize that Savior wherever he appears again.

Jacob: Broken and Clinging to God

There is no greater sickness than the illusion that we can save ourselves if we work hard. Jacob believed deeply that you must hustle if you are going to make something of your life. My hunch is that Jacob was the first person to coin the phrase "God helps those who help themselves." It isn't a biblical phrase, but if it were, Jacob would have said it.

The word *Jacob* means supplanter, schemer, hustler. That turned out to be appropriate because from day one Jacob was focused on achieving all of the blessings in life that naturally fell on Esau.

Esau was not complicated. Maybe that was because life had never been too hard on him. Esau is one of those persons who seem to have been born right. He is like those today who just find themselves successful and don't know what to do with it all. Esau drives us crazy. No one was plagued by Esau more than Jacob, who spent his early life running a con on his older brother.

The story of these two brothers is not unique. It is the story of the haves and the have-nots. It is the story of those whose lives seem dreamlike and those who spend their lives chasing dreams. It is not unlike the story of our lives. Some of us may be able to relate to Esau, but most of us find ourselves rooting for Jacob. We like his drive. The odds are against him, but he is determined to make something of himself. Jacob's story is our story.

There is an important quirk in this narrative, however. Before Jacob was born, God decided to bless him, not Esau. In the Old Testament, to be blessed by God meant to be chosen for a special purpose and mission in life. That blessing was offered earlier to Jacob's grandfather Abraham. He wanted that blessing so much that he was willing to leave his home to chase after the dreams God was offering. When Isaac was born, rather late in the game, Abraham was already beginning to realize that the blessing was not in receiving his dreams but in living with the gracious God who provides them.

Those lessons of faith were lost on Jacob. For him, what you see is what you get. And in spite of God's promise to bless Jacob, he didn't see any evidence of it. Throughout his life Jacob kept hearing from God about his blessings. In Genesis 32:9 it comes in its most simple form, "I will do you good."

Blessings in those days came as birthrights. As the second born, our man was born wrong. So Jacob has his doubts about God. He doesn't doubt the blessing. That he takes very seriously. What he doubts is that it will be a blessing for him.

Most of us have some doubts about God. When we read in the newspaper that whole nations are starving to death, we sometimes have doubts about the kingdom that Jesus said would be coming. In the course of our daily lives, though, we don't spend a great deal of time struggling over such big questions. Mostly, what we doubt is that our own lives will add up to much if we stop running and hustling. We doubt that grace will pull through in the end to change the way it is for us.

When these doubts appear, the great temptation is for us to turn the blessing of God into ambitious goals that we will get for ourselves. If any blessings are going to come our way, we who can get the job done are going to have to help God out. Because, we know, there are Jacobs and there are Esaus in the world. There are those who seem to have it made and those who are going to have to make it happen. So we look desperately to our careers, wealth, families, friends and church. We hope that if we work hard enough in these areas, we can make a blessing happen.

The problem with hustling to help God out is that we usually end up tired and beaten by the way it is. No one illustrates this better than Jacob. By the time we catch up to the story in Genesis 32, Jacob is alone and broken. In his desperation to find a blessing he has lost his family and his money, his homeland and everything he has achieved through hard work. He had to run to Laban, his father-in-law, to get away from Esau. Now that he is on the run from Laban, the only place to go is back to Esau, who is still out to get him for stealing the birthright.

Now it is all caving in on him. There are no more new towns to move to, no more new jobs to start, no more wives to marry. He is all out of opportunities for self-improvement. In verse 24 we are told that Jacob is left alone, abandoned by everything.

Actually, Jacob had been alone throughout his life. He lived more with the absence of God than with his grace. In his lonely, defeated exhaustion, Jacob spent the night wrestling with God. It is symbolic of the struggle of his life. Jacob and God had been wrestling for a long, long time.

This is the struggle of those who believe in the blessing but are fighting to keep believing, to keep doubt from overcoming them and to hold on to the promise that God will do them good. It is a good struggle in that it illustrates the integrity of those who take God's blessing too seriously to ignore the contradictions of reality. If we simply didn't believe in the blessing, there would be no struggle. We would simply fall into the nihilistic absurdity of life that characterizes the beliefs of so many in society who are trying to account for life's abandonments.

In the course of this great wrestling match, Jacob's hip is thrown out of joint. What could be worse for a hustler? It cripples him and ends his days of hard running. The striking thing is that he hangs onto this messenger from God and refuses to let go until he gets his blessing. That image of the broken, exhausted Jacob, hanging onto his embrace of God, portrays the final position of faith. Here is a timeless illustration of all who have taken the blessing seriously and tried hard to make it happen. They end with empty hands and crippled legs so that they must hold on to God. Because, at last, there is nothing else to do.

At daybreak the blessing finally comes. It is not quite the blessing Jacob had been trying to pull off. He did not receive wealth, esteem or the success of Esau. His healing did not repair the painful hip. But he was healed, blessed with a new name. No longer would he be known as the hustler. Now he is to be called Israel, which means "those who struggle with God." "Your name shall be Israel, for you have striven with God, and with others, and have prevailed" (see Genesis 32:27-28).

Prevailed? How has this abandoned, crippled hustler prevailed? He received the blessing, the identity, of one who took God seriously and struggled to make sense of his promises. It is a rather dangerous thing to wrestle with God, but that has been the blessing all along. In that struggle he found his life.

Israel is, of course, the name of a whole people who have

struggled with God for centuries. Those are people of faith, who frequently get a little beaten up because they are not always certain about God. So it has always been for a people of faith.

We are not a people who are miraculously changed into Esaus because God likes us. That is what we would like faith to do. We would like for faith to help us in our crusades to get the life of our dreams. But that is not the purpose of faith. We do not live by faith in God's intervention. We live by faith in God's grace when there is no intervention.

As the prophets of Israel illustrate, faith means asking questions. This struggle has to be encouraged. It is part of our identity. It is what it means to live by faith. Our churches are loaded with people who are struggling with serious health issues, with families that seem to be coming apart at the seams and with jobs that they hate but don't dare leave. Christians in other parts of the world struggle with poverty, violence and oppressive governments. And we just have to wonder why. Why?

We dare not shrug that question away, not if we are a people of faith. Every abandonment is the invitation to strive with God. When the wrestling was over for Jacob nothing had really changed, but everything was different. He realized he had seen God face to face. It was all he needed. From that moment, he made peace with life.

As we struggle to understand and fearfully take God on, the promise is that we too will see his face. He does not give us the things we want. He does not give us explanations. He just gives us himself. In the church we call that discovery worship. And that, we believe, is the purpose of life.

6

Abandoned by Family

JESUS STILL CALLS HIS DISCIPLES away from families where they think they belong. After they abandon all claims to family, their lives become lonely and empty—empty enough to be filled with God's gift of a new family. This is not their dream of what family would be like; rather, it is the real family of God called the church.

Shoes That Cannot Be Filled

One Saturday afternoon the fellowship hall of our church was filled with people milling around tables stacked high with old clothes. The Women's Association of the church was having its annual clothing sale to raise money for missions. I was enjoying walking around the room as I chatted with our different members who were working hard but having a good time. Then I noticed Helen, recently widowed after almost sixty years of marriage.

One look at her face made it clear that she was not having an easy time. Her eyes were moist as she told me, "My husband always took such good care of his shoes. He would polish them every night and then carefully place them under our bed so they would be ready to wear in the morning. I just found them on a table where they were being sold for three dollars."

I have talked to Helen several times since Dick, her husband, died. Like many widows, she is making her way through the long days of grief as well as she can. What she worries about the most is not the grief but preserving the memories. She is worried that we will forget the incalculable value of the man who once wore those shoes.

Remembering is an important gift for a church to give. The bereaved want us never to forget that their loved ones were special people. They want us to miss them and cherish the lives they lived. It is for this reason that so many old churches have little brass plaques nailed onto pews and windows with the names of people who died long ago. Their family members tried to nail down memories of them in their church. It helps with the grief to think that others may remember when they sit on that pew or pass that window. It is as if these plaques whisper in church, "Don't forget."

That is an important gift, but it is not the best gift the church brings to the bereaved. The best gift is that we become for them the body of Christ. Sometimes that means the church is the "man of sorrows." Right after a death, church members surround the family and join in their tears. They bring covered dishes to the house, and they offer their eulogies at the funeral. As Christ carries our burdens, so does the church carry some of the grief. We feel the hurt. We ache over the death of somebody's loved one as if it were our family member who had died, which it was.

In time, also as the body of Christ, the church becomes the

"good shepherd." We lead those lost in their grief out of the chaos that immediately follows death and give them a vision for the still waters of peace. We do this every Sunday when the church stands and confesses its belief in the resurrection from the dead and in the life to come. We do it every time we baptize a new baby which offers the gentle reminder that as the Lord taketh away, so does the Lord give. We do it when we ask a veteran of grief to make a call on someone whose loved one has just died.

Eventually those in grief discover that the Good Shepherd has "restored their souls." The loved one who died is not forgotten and will always be missed. As it did for Helen, a day will come when the bereaved realize they are able to go on with their lives. But they won't be the same. They aren't better or worse. They are just different. They are new creations. The world seems a little different for them now, and their God seems very different. The grief has converted their lives. It has turned them around. Now they see a side of life, and a side of God, that can be seen only by those who have lost someone who was so very dear. Now they look to the Good Shepherd who alone can lead them through the dark and lonely nights of grief.

Are There Broken Families?

Death isn't the only way we lose the families of our dreams. Divorce is another. Sometimes it is even harder than death. The church doesn't know what to do for someone who goes through a divorce. There is no tearful memorial service. No one shows up at the door with dinner. Friends may feel clumsy and fear saying the wrong thing. So they say nothing at all.

Divorce is wrong. No one believes that more than people who have gone through it. There is no question in my mind that divorce is a sin. But I agonize over how to bring a ministry of grace into the lives of those who have been torn apart by this failure. Like death, divorce isn't something that people get over. The broken heart may eventually heal, but the scars remain. The hurt of the divorced is deep. When children are involved, the hurt just keeps hurting.

The hurt is great for the father as well as the mother. But since it is typically the mother who ends up with primary custody of the children, I have witnessed more of the trials of single parenting from her perspective.

I am amazed at her courage in taking on enormous obstacles every day. She alone is responsible for getting the kids up, dressed and off to school. Every morning she says a quiet prayer that no one will wake up sick. If things go well, she makes it to work on time and puts in just as arduous a day as those who have spouses waiting for them at home. But when she gets home, she is the one who has to prepare dinner for the family. But dinner is a long way off after work is done. First she has to stop by the place where she pays out an enormous percentage of her salary for childcare. Then she stops by the grocery and maybe the cleaners or the veterinarian to pick up a sick dog. After dinner is finally done, and the arguments over whose turn it is to do the dishes have been mediated, this lone parent then tries to help with homework and get the kids bathed and ready for bed. After a story and a prayer, she tucks each cherished child into bed with reminders that she loves them and that she will never leave them. With the few precious moments left she pays some bills, does the wash, calls her parents to see how they are doing and then gets ready for the next day—when it will all start again. But as challenging as all of that is, it isn't the hardest part of her single life.

The hard part is coping with the abandonment of the dreams she had about her family. This is not the life she was thinking about so many years ago when she walked down the aisle to meet her husband at the altar. But it is the life she has. She would like to put "him" out of her life these days. Were it not for the children, that might be possible. But he is usually involved with them at some level, even if it is only financial. More important, and this may be the hardest of all, she knows she has to raise her children to love the man who hurt her. It is so tempting to turn the children against their father, and it isn't as if she doesn't have plenty of ammunition to give them. But she knows that would harm them.

If she is fortunate, she has found a counselor and a support group where it is safe to talk about him. In spite of her protests about making ends meet, they will caution her that she is working so hard at life as a way of avoiding her feelings. But when she is alone in bed late at night, the feelings and the tears know where to find her. *I'm incredibly busy,* she tells herself. *How can I feel so lonely?*

Some of these women dream of meeting another man one day who will take away the loneliness. Others have seen too many discouraging statistics about divorced mothers getting remarried to hold on to that hope. Many have watched their friends marry divorced men with children and have become discouraged by the new set of issues blended families take on. After a while, many single women don't know what to hope for. It is at that point that they need the church. They need it to be a place where the words *grace* and *hope* are mentioned. Even more, they need it to be their new family where their brokenness is shared—shared to the point that they are no longer unique as a broken family.

At church all of our families are broken. Even in those families where Mom and Dad still love each other, there has been enough hurt to shatter the illusion that they don't need the grace of God to stay together. If the church limits its ministry to holding up the "ideal family," it will miss its great opportunity to participate in God's conversion of those who long ago were abandoned by their ideals. At that point the church will cease being the body of Christ, for Jesus made it clear that he came to heal the broken. When Jesus was judged by the righteous for spending too much time with sinners, he responded by saying, "Those who are well have no need of a physician, but those who are sick; I have come to call not the righteous but sinners" (Mark 2:17).

The New Family

I have often wondered how surprised Jesus' family must have been when he left home to begin his ministry. He was the oldest son in a possibly fatherless home. He abandoned the normal expectations of any family in his day. Everyone would have expected him to stay home, tend to the carpenter's shop and take care of his mother.

We are told about a time during Jesus' ministry when his family came to see him. He had been preaching to "the crowds" when his mother and brothers asked if they could talk to him. But when someone told him that his family was standing outside wanting to speak to him, Jesus replied, "Who is my mother, and who are my brothers?" Then, pointing to the disciples, he said, "Here are my mother and my brothers! For whoever does the will of my Father in heaven is my brother and sister and mother" (Matthew 12:48-50). Jesus was not dismissing his family's importance, as he continued to care for them right up to the time he was on the cross. However, with those words he established a new family that, created by the heavenly Father, had now become the first family in his life.

This is much more radical than most Christians want to admit. We are accustomed to hearing speakers remind us that our first priority in life is to God, our second is to our families and our third is to the ministry God has given us. But that hierarchy is hard to find in the Bible. The New Testament in particular has a very different understanding of family from that which has emerged in the late twentieth century. It does very little to assure us that right behind our devotion to God comes a loyalty to the two-parent, two-child model we now assume is the all-American family.[1] Rather it tells us all too clearly that if we do the will of the Father, we are given a new family made up of those who share this same Father. What we now call the nuclear family may or may not be a part of that new family. It all depends on who is the real Father of the family.

At our church we explain this to families that don't look like the all-American model. They are thrilled to learn that there is a new model. It means that they are no longer destined to go through life as failed approximations of families that have two parents. They have joined others who came to the church because they too knew they needed a savior, and thus they have become a part of our family. They join singles who never married, old folks who were widowed long ago and couples who have not produced children. Together they become a real family. Of course this is a spiritual family, but that is the most real family there is.

The church turns us into grandparents, sons and daughters, mothers and fathers. For those who live far from biological grandparents, the church offers the maturing, stabilizing influence of an older generation that is invested in the lives of our children. In our congregation when a teenager got very sick and had to go the hospital repeatedly for treatment, it was the older folks who took turns taking her back and forth, as if they were in fact her grandparents. We have a single woman who goes to a nursing home every week to visit the mother of someone who lives far away. Over the years that relationship has grown so close that I wonder who is the real daughter. We have a man who has assumed the responsibility of caring for young adults who lost their jobs in our city. He helps them a bit with advice and financial management, but mostly he is just the stabilizing influence of a white-haired father who says, "Don't worry, everything is going to be OK." Typically that is all they need. If someone asked these caregivers about their "ministry" at church, they would say they are just taking care of each other. I try to remind them that taking care of each other is our family business.

When we tell the two-parent families about the priority of the family of God, they either rejoice or become quite anxious. If they have told the truth, really told the truth, about their families being just as needy, they rejoice in being a part of the new family of God. If they are still under the illusion that church is a place where they come to learn the secrets to a better marriage, or the place that offers a youth group so their kids are protected from the influences of secular high schools, then they are not so happy to hear about joining needy siblings in the one family of God. Our best ministry to these folks is to avoid giving them the false assurances they crave. It is not until they realize that their families are also broken that any real ministry of grace can begin.

Dietrich Bonhoeffer was careful to remind us that the church is not a human ideal, but it is a divine reality.[2] Our dreams of community, he cautioned, are the greatest threat to true Christian community. It is God's family that we find in the church. This is not necessarily a better family than the one we left. It is certainly not the family of our dreams. It is a holy family, but that is only because God is our Father. In my church family we ask people to be careful with each other, but the truth is that we fight and hurt each other as much as any family on earth. We have to do a whole lot of asking and receiving of forgiveness. But that is part of our distinctiveness as a family. We know how to forgive. That too is our family business.

It is amazing how many good organizations there are in Washington, D.C., that are working hard to make the world a better place. Some of these are lobbyists, others are government agencies, others are nonprofit groups that exist to respond to a particular need. All of them share a common understanding of right and wrong. They are certain that their cause is right. They exist to go out from their group and fight the enemy—poverty, crime, injustice, pollution. But the enemy is always out there.

The church is so different from these organizations. For us, the enemy is inside the church. The enemy is at work in every one of our hearts. We do not engage in mission or evangelism to the other families of the earth because we are a superior alternative. What makes our family different? We know how much we need a savior. It is as we meet the Savior in the family, as we receive his forgiveness and learn the art of forgiving, that we discover something worth offering to those outside of the family. That is particularly important for those who are dealing with unresolved issues with their parents.

Honor Thy Father and Mother

Many today are engaging in courageous therapeutic journeys that invite them to return to unresolved issues in their past. These are not easy journeys, and most of us would rather just leave the past in the past. But it doesn't stay there. Those who do not understand the influence of old hurts are destined to be haunted by them. These unresolved issues will continue to complicate their lives.

We have to tell the truth about the hurt that was part of our parents' legacy. But what of the Fifth Commandment that directs us to "honor thy father and mother"? Does this commandment say that we are self-indulgent in looking at wounds from parents who were too busy, too strict and too hurt themselves to give us the love we craved? Or does the commandment to honor father and mother just apply to those many parents who did an honorable job and knocked themselves out with love for their kids? The answer to both of these questions is no.

It is not wrong to tell the truth about what was done and left undone so long ago. But this commandment is not conditional. We are not told to honor only those parents who do well at parenting. We are told to "honor your father and your mother, so that your days may be long in the land that the LORD your God is giving you" (Exodus 20:12).

This is the first of the Ten Commandments that comes with a promise. If we honor our parents, our days will be long in the new place to which the Lord is leading. The promise reminds us that we are on a journey. As the Hebrews journeyed between Egypt and the Promised Land, so do we as God's people continue to journey between a former place and a new place, between a former family and a new family.

Clearly, in commanding us to honor parents the Bible does not tell us to avoid the journey to the new family. However, it does caution us that unless we honor the family from which we came, we will never be able to receive the family to which we are heading. At least, not for long.

We are not told to stay at home with father and mother, to agree with father and mother or to assume the values of father and mother. In fact, we are not even told to love father and mother.

What we are told is that we must honor them. To honor means to esteem something for the significance it has. We honor parents when we realize we did not spring forth out of nothing. Our lives were shaped by those who raised us. Some of them did that so well. Others were just awful at it. But in either case unless we honor the influence they have borne in our lives, we will never be free to receive the future. All of life will be spent in angry reaction, searching for the mythical better family.

It could be that the flaws of father and mother are our best preparation for receiving the flawed relationships of the future. For those who believe Mom and Dad did a pretty good job, the most honorable way to say thanks is to get on with the task of leaving them and cleaving to another.

Life is not something we create. It's something we receive, created by God. Both the pain and the joy are creative. Both must be honored as the experiences that mold our lives. Nowhere is that more obvious than in family life.

At the conclusion of a university graduation ceremony I once saw a robed doctoral candidate standing on the steps of a great Gothic chapel. In his arms he was holding his young son. Beside him stood his parents. Beside them was a grandparent. Four generations were smiling for the photograph on one day of glory. That photograph probably sits framed on someone's mantel as a priceless treasure. But we will have to look more closely to see all the ordinary days that lie behind that picture.

There was that day long ago when his grandmother put him on her lap and read their favorite story, tracing his little finger around each letter. Later there were many days when his mother sat with him at the kitchen table patiently explaining long division. Then came the day his dad drove him to college. Although everyone has tried hard to forget it, they can still remember the day he got into that awful fight with his folks. He said they were just smothering him with rules and didn't understand that he was an adult now. He would live his own life. His father stormed out of the room. His mother cried. Chances are no one took pictures then.

Year by year ordinary days piled up, one after the other. Some of them were happy. Some were not. But through them all a life was created and then allowed to go its own way. Those who have learned to receive their life and leave behind the illusion that they created it for themselves find it easier to honor the parent as one of God's primary methods for molding their life.

This is no less true for families that were unhealthy. In those cases the best way to honor father and mother is to forgive them. This is the only path from old hurts to a new life. In the words of novelist Anne Lamott, "Forgiveness is giving up all hope of having a better past."[3] The invitation of God is to be converted out of the past, especially the past we did not create. We may think that holding on to the hurt is a way of judging our parents, but actually it is just a way of refusing to accept responsibility for the future.

Joseph: God Intended It for Good

There are few families more dysfunctional than the one in which Joseph was raised. He was the eleventh of Jacob's twelve sons. His father tried to love him but did not know how. Jacob showered Joseph with gifts because he loved his youngest two sons more than the other ten children. Eventually the older half brothers got fed up with Daddy's favorite. So they sold Joseph into slavery.

After an extended, pain-filled adventure in losing his life, Joseph found a new life as the trusted assistant of the pharaoh of Egypt. He was responsible for the grain storehouses. During a severe famine the brothers came to Egypt to buy grain, and whom did they have to depend on for mercy but Joseph! When they confessed their sin to him, he was able to forgive them only because he had seen how God's conversion had been evident in his life—even through their evil.

This does not mean that God caused the brothers to do him harm, but it does mean that no evil is too great for God to redeem. Had the brothers not sold Joseph into slavery, he would not have been in a position to save the covenant people of God from famine. As Joseph told his brothers, "Even though you intended to do harm to me, God intended it for good, in order to preserve a numerous people, as he is doing today" (Genesis 50:20).

The best place to find a redemptive use for the hurt created by our families is in the new family of God, the church. It is in the new family that we discover our Christian vocation, what God is calling us to do with life. Typically, that calling is heard through many discoveries of oneself, not the least of which is the discovery that God has intended good for us even through the harm done by others. The good intention of God is that through these hurts, not in spite of them, we will be his instruments of care in the lives of others.

The best counselors of the bereaved in our church are those who have laid members of their family into the arms of God. They know something about grief because they have been there themselves. For example, they never say "I know how you feel," because veterans know how lonely grief is. They understand that no one but the person who is left really knows what it feels like to have lost this particular loved one.

The best care for those who are going through divorce is provided by a community of other divorced people in the church. The best care for those with codependency issues is to work out their recovery with others who are only a few steps ahead on the same journey. The same redemptive fellowship of suffering awaits those who were abused in childhood, those who have very sick children and those who cope with mental illness in their families.

It is even true that our ability to recover from grief or to forgive our families of origin is directly related to our discovery of vocation in the new family. It was as Joseph saw the good intentions of God that he was able to forgive, or release, his brothers from the harm they did him. Forgiveness apart from some vision of the purposes of God is asking too much. Receiving a vision for the purposes of God apart from the Christian family is not possible.

Abandoned by Our Dreams of Family

Mary is a delightful, very attractive, forty-five-year-old single woman in our congregation who has never been married. She has been successful in her career with the federal government and is deeply loved by many in our church. She owns her own home, drives a beautiful car, travels a great deal and has met all the great aspirations she had when she left college. All except one. She did not became a mother, and now she thinks she never will.

It bothers her more than she admits. She would trade all of her success and freedom for a family in a minute. But she doesn't say that too often. To admit that she would give it all up for a husband and children sounds as if she made a mistake in her life choices. She and many other women have worked too hard to achieve what they have in their careers. There was a day when women were not allowed to attain her level of professional success, and she is not about to contribute to any reactionary effort to return to the old days when a woman's place was confined to the home. Still, more than anything, she would love to have a family. She remembers choosing a profession, but she never chose to be single.

Mary left college determined to have both a career and a family. She assumed that she would eventually find the right guy and get married. She expected that they would figure out how to have children and raise them in a loving home while continuing their careers. Lots of other women were doing this, and there was no reason to think she couldn't do it as well. She dated a lot through her twenties and thirties, but the right guy never came along. In the meantime, she threw herself into her career and continued to wait on the Lord's timing for marriage. The Lord's timing has been slow.

Mary is illustrative of a great many single women in our church who are approaching middle age. Their biological clocks have rung off the wall, and they are now grieving the abandonment of their dreams for family. Some of them are still hoping for marriage, but many have decided that even if that happens it is too late to have children.

We also have a number of men in the congregation who are in the same boat, but for reasons I don't fully understand, it is different for them. Most of our single men don't share the grief experienced by our single women. Maybe that is because they think they have more time to get around to family. Maybe it's because in spite of all our social progress with women, men still have the privilege of deciding when to ask a woman to get married. In her more cynical moments, Mary says that the men who wanted relationships are all married by now.

Something happened to Mary shortly after her dream died. A great sadness settled into her life. She continued to go about her work and her many activities at church, but the gleam that used to be in her eye faded. She began to see a counselor. After spending a considerable amount of time in therapy, she concluded that her problem wasn't depression or anything clinical. It was more like despair and the loss of hope. That made it a spiritual issue.

What Can We Count On in a Savior?

Losing hope is essentially another way of saying that we have lost our vision of the Savior. We can no longer see him at work in our lives. As long as we are certain that Jesus is with us, we know that anything can happen. The Gospels are full of accounts of his miracle-working power, but the greatest miracle is that in Jesus God finds those of us who have lost not only our dreams but our lives. As long as we can see that the Savior is with us, we are not lost. But if we have focused too narrowly on the dream we thought the savior would give us, then it is the dream that has become the savior and not Jesus.

None of our dreams will get us back to God. Only Jesus will do that. And getting us back to God is the only thing we can be sure Jesus wants to do. It is the only thing that will save our lives, even if we have to be cut free from our dreams. Perhaps it was for this reason that Jesus said,

I have not come to bring peace, but a sword.
For I have come to set a man against his father,
and a daughter against her mother,
and a daughter-in-law against her mother-in-law;
and one's foes will be members of one's own household.
Whoever loves father or mother more than me is not worthy of me; and whoever loves son or daughter more than me is not worthy of me; and whoever does not take up the cross and follow me is not worthy of me. (Matthew 10:34-38)

This passage is harsh. Most of us are knocking ourselves out to do everything we can to keep the family taped together in these days of soaring divorce statistics. At first glance, it does not seem that Jesus and his sword are going to help return the American family to its place of esteemed sanctity in society. And if we stay with this passage awhile and study it carefully, we become convinced that our first impression was right. Jesus is not going to ensure that the family is honored. Nor will he ensure that the church is honored, or that our nation is honored, or any other thing we want to put on his agenda as a Savior.

This is not to say that the family or these other institutions are unimportant. In fact, there is much in the Bible that calls us to conduct our relationships in them in a way that honors

God. But that is the important difference between the Bible and our dreams. What is it that we must honor? Is it the family, or the God who may or may not give us that family as the opportunity to honor him? God alone is the object of our worship, and we can count on Jesus to save us from anything that becomes an idol in God's place. That includes our dreams for family.

It is hard to base our hope simply on the mysterious and often invisible work of Jesus in our lives. It is harder yet to really believe that it would be a good thing for Jesus to save us from our dreams.

In my pastoral care of Mary we have spent a lot of time talking about her prayers. For so long she had prayed for God to help her find her dreams. During the despair that she experienced when she realized that she wasn't going to get those dreams, she prayed angry, tearful prayers of lament. My task was not to tell her what to pray, but just to keep her talking to God. I assured her that God has the self-esteem to handle her anger. She prayed to understand her God. She asked over and over if he was really a good God, if he really loved her, if he even remembered who she was. The next turning point came when she found she was simply praying for God himself. By then her dreams seemed far less important than her relationship to the Savior. In time she developed a passion to simply "be" with her God, every day. Of course that was God's dream all along.

Jesus Had Bad Holidays Too

There is no time that family dreams and reality collide quite like Christmas. Christmas is the judgment day of family life. The dynamics that make our families what they are all year somehow get multiplied exponentially at the holidays. Things that have been mildly irritating all year become crises about this time. The things about family that have always been a quiet strength will now become our great hope for a truly merry Christmas. Since most families have both irritating and joyful dimensions to them, it only makes sense that we then experience the lowest of our lows and the highest of our highs. If nothing else, we can count on Christmas to be dramatic.

Good or bad, it comes around every year. Some dread the holiday because their families don't hold up too well under its pressures. All the thin veneer is ripped off if the family has pasted anything over the truth.

Those who have undergone divorce or a death in the family simply try to survive the season's expectations of joy. Many can't even set up the Christmas tree because they know someone's present will not be under it this year.

The people who worry their pastors the most are the ones who think this is the year the family will change and do Christmas right. As they express these dreams to me, I am always tempted to ask, "Is this the same family you had last year? Why will they be different?" But year after year, they expect their family to magically turn into the dreams that have taken a beating all year.

The church is in the wonderful position of seeing these family dynamics from the perspective of various ages. Once at a church gathering that was held a couple of weeks before Christmas, some of our younger members talked openly about their fear of going "home" for the holidays. "There is so much pretense in my home," one young man said. "We have never dealt with my father's drinking problem or my mother's life-long passive-aggressive demeanor. Then at Christmas we are supposed to stand around the family piano and sing carols as if we were a happy family." Several other young people sighed as if they knew the scenario all too well. Then an old couple spoke up. The father said, "Our daughter will bring her family home in a couple of weeks, and to tell you the truth we are scared of what will happen. We love her more than she knows, and we can't wait to see the grandkids. But ever since she has been in counseling, she always comes home angry. I know we're going to end up having another one of her 'talks' where she dredges up all our mistakes as parents. I'm tired of being the reason her life isn't happy. Why can't we just enjoy the little time we have together?"

I wonder if these two generations have heard each other. The church has been for them the substitute family where it is possible to say what biological family members have a hard time telling each other. When these stories are intertwined with biblical stories, it is possible for real hope to emerge.

In all four of the Gospels there is only one account of Jesus' life during the formative years of early adolescence. It is a profound story of what happened at a holiday when he was twelve years old and he wasn't where he was supposed to be. It provided yet another illustration for Jesus' mother that there could be no salvation until she abandoned her expectations regarding her family.

It was Passover, a time when Jews made a great pilgrimage to Jerusalem to remember their deliverance from slavery. Every year Joseph and Mary took their son to Jerusalem for this event. Certainly they told him the great story of the exodus every year. They told him it was God's business to deliver people from slavery. They told him the Jews were waiting for another deliverer—a messiah who would save the people who had again lost their way.

After his twelfth birthday, Jesus was considered a man by the Jewish tradition. He was expected to take the Passover and the hope for a messiah very seriously. He did. That is why the problem began. After the holiday was over, the people from Nazareth started for home. To their horror, a day into the trip,

Mary and Joseph discovered that their son was missing. It was not uncommon for a boy his age to be with other boys his age. He had made the trip before. He was old enough to know that it was his responsibility to be on the caravan. Maybe they had even worked on the "responsibility" thing.

What follows, after the discovery that Joseph and Mary had lost Jesus, is a fascinating journey in emotions. First came anxiety, maybe even panic. For three of the longest days in their lives they searched all over Jerusalem. It was a big city. There were lots of places for a boy to get in trouble. Next came astonishment, when his parents finally discovered him alive and well in the temple. Who would expect to find a twelve-year-old kid in a place of worship, talking with the clergy, doing theology? It was astonishing.

But something snapped in Mary. Some parent chromosome kicked in, and astonishment gave way to anger. She said, "Child [she wasn't taking this twelve-year-old man concept too seriously], why have you treated us like this? Look, your father and I have been searching for you in great anxiety" (Luke 2:48). It was as if she had asked, "Jesus, why weren't you where you were supposed to be?"

From fear to astonishment to anger. It is a journey many of us have taken with Jesus. Having sung the songs of Christmas and read the stories about the birth of our hope for one more year, we return to "real life" as if nothing life-changing had occurred. The holiday is over. Jobs and responsibilities are waiting. The family can go back to being whatever it is eleven and a half months a year. It is time to set out on the road back to normal. We expect Jesus to be on that road with us. Even if we can't see him every day, we assume he is near. It would be terrifying to discover that he is not as near as we thought.

If we lose sight of God's salvation in our families, we can try to find Jesus in many places. We can look for him in our dreams of what will happen when the family gathers for the next holiday. We can look for him by turning away from family and rushing back to work. Once we have discovered something very important is missing from our families, we, like Mary and Joseph, can search all over the city for our hope. Maybe we will find it in a different church youth group, or a new therapist, or a bigger house. But we cannot find our savior in any of them, and the search continues.

When we do stumble into the place where Jesus is, we are always astonished. Salvation never occurs as we expect. Ironically, it is usually our expectations that keep us from seeing Jesus. Parents are astonished to find Jesus with their children. Children are even more astonished to find him with their parents. Those who have always had wonderful families will be astonished to find Jesus when family life takes a turn for the worse. Those who have grown accustomed to bad families will be astonished to discover Jesus can heal. According to the text, Jesus is not where we thought he should be. That's enough to make us angry. In Mary's words, "Jesus, why have you done this to us?" In our words, "Jesus, why didn't you save my marriage? Jesus, why didn't you rescue my father from his disease? Jesus, I have been searching for you in great anxiety!"

Jesus' response to this is striking. "Why were you searching for me? Did you not know that I must be in my Father's house?" It is as if to say, "Why would you have to search? Don't you know that I'll be about the business of salvation?" Usually it is not until we give up searching for Jesus in the places where we expected him to be that we make an astonishing discovery. There is more to God than we know. He has more business, more conversion, with our lives than we have received.

Mary's final response is recorded for us. She did not stay angry. We are told that she "treasured all these things in her heart." It was the same response she made to the story of the shepherds when Jesus was born. She took to heart an experience she did not fully understand.

There would be a lot of that for Mary. It culminated on a Passover twenty-one years later, when she found her son on a cross. It was another place he was not supposed to be. But it was the place where the business of God was being done and where our salvation occurred. That is, if we have leaned into it, if we have taken it to heart.

That is an important story for the church to tell itself over and over. It reminds us that even in the new family, especially in the new family, our Savior will not be predictable. He is too concerned with our salvation to stay in the places the church expects him to be. If we are certain that he is primarily concerned with our own family life, we will be startled to find him at work outside of the church. If we are convinced that he is only the Savior of society's poor, we will be startled to find him in love with the materialistic institutional church. About the only thing we can predict is that he will be looking for those in need of a savior. When he finds them, before he even cleans them up and gives them the right theology, he calls them our brothers and sisters. That's his business. That makes it ours as well.

7
Abandoned by God

THE DEEP FEAR LYING BEHIND EVERY loss is that we have been abandoned by the God who should have saved us. The transforming moment in Christian conversion comes when we realize that even God has left us. We then discover it was not God, but our image of God, that abandoned us. This frees us to discover more of the mystery of God than we knew. Only then is change possible.

When Jesus Is Too Late
We don't tend to think that Jesus had ordinary relationships and friends. We know that disciples followed him all over Israel. There were all kinds of people around him who needed healing, food and answers to life. But these were not the kind of friends who drop by for dinner. However, Scripture indicates that he did indeed have close friends. Among them were Mary, Martha and their brother Lazarus. He went to their house often.

Apparently he stayed with them whenever he was in Bethany. "Jesus loved" this family (John 11:5).

One day when Jesus was not in Bethany, his friend Lazarus became gravely sick. The sisters sent word to Jesus saying, "Lord, he whom you love is ill" (John 11:3). Jesus' response to their message is fascinating. The New King James Version reads, "Now Jesus loved Martha and her sister and Lazarus. *So,* when He heard that he was sick, He stayed two more days in the place where He was" (John 11:5). It was *because* Jesus loved this family that he did not rush to save Lazarus.

This is the reverse of how we would expect Jesus to demonstrate his love. Why didn't Jesus hurry to take care of his friend? How can loving Lazarus be a reason for Jesus to abandon him? Perhaps it is because as God in the flesh, Jesus is illustrating once again that God's ways of loving are not our ways. For example, Jesus never hurries.

When Jesus did arrive, he found that Lazarus had already been in the tomb four days. The Savior showed up late. Too late. Now Lazarus is dead. Things have gone from bad to hopeless.

Sometimes life gets overwhelming, and we realize we could use a little help. So we pray for our health to get better, for our marriage to work out, for success in our work that has taken a turn for the worse. There is nothing wrong in praying for these things, but they are not what our salvation is about. Don't expect Jesus to save us by teaching us to depend on the things we are afraid of losing. He loves us too much to let our health, marriage or work become the savior of our lives. He will abandon every crusade that searches for salvation from anything or anyone other than God. So he delays, he watches as we race down dead-end streets, he lets our mission du jour crash and burn.

To receive Jesus as Savior means recognizing him as our

only help. Not our only help for getting what we want. But our only true help. When we ask for a savior, we are not asking for a boost. We are asking for a miracle. We cannot discover that miracle until Lazarus is dead, the marriage is over, the job lost or the health gone. What we were so afraid of happening has happened. Jesus abandoned us in our time of need.

When Martha heard that Jesus was coming, she left Mary at home and ran down the road to meet him. "Jesus," she says, "if only you had been here, my brother would not have died." Jesus responds, "Martha, your brother will rise again." The grief-stricken sister wipes away some tears, sighs and says, "I know that he will rise again in the resurrection on the last day" (see John 11:20-24).

It is fascinating that four days into her grief, after Jesus finally showed up, Martha started discussing her beliefs with him. I see this all the time. When a pastor gets a call to "come quickly to the hospital; he is about to die," often the family talks like Martha. They do not seem interested in discussing the depths of their grief. They just want me to remind them of what they already know, what they have rehearsed in church Sunday after Sunday.

The LORD *is* my shepherd;
  I shall not want. . . .
Yea, though I walk through the valley of the shadow of death,
  I will fear no evil. . . .

I believe in God the Father Almighty,
  Maker of heaven and earth,
  and in Jesus Christ his only Son our Lord. . . .
I believe in the resurrection of the body
  and the life everlasting.

125

As Martha returned to one of these belief statements, Jesus interrupted her to say, "I am the resurrection and the life. . . . Do you believe this?" (John 11:25-26).

For years and years we sit through sermon after sermon. We can recite Scripture from memory. We know a lot about the faith, and we easily call Jesus the resurrection and the life. But for every one of us there comes a time when Jesus interrupts us to ask, "Do you believe this? Do you believe in what you know?" It makes all the difference when your Lazarus dies, because then belief is all you have.

When Lazarus dies, we are thrown into darker, more naked belief, belief that is not clothed in anything that gives us comfort. This is belief as real faith. It is a faith that simply hangs on the cross of Jesus while everything else drops off. Faith is what binds us to Christ when everything is gone, including our most cherished expectations of him.

This leaves us with less intellectual content to our faith, but with a whole lot more love for the Savior. On the other side of death we discover that it is not what we know that saves us but who we love, and even more important, who we believe loves us. So the real question for people of faith is "Do we believe we are loved by a Savior?" This belief is enough to see us through; indeed, believing in his love for us may be all we have.

"Yes, Lord," Martha said. "I believe you are the Messiah, the Savior" (see John 11:27). Later in the text it becomes obvious that she doesn't entirely understand what that means. But that's OK. Who can predict what it means that Jesus will save us? Who predicted Easter? For now, it is enough to simply believe in Jesus.

When Martha's sister, Mary, reached Jesus, they didn't talk theology. They just cried. It is striking that she also says that Lazarus would have been fine if only Jesus had not delayed.

Both sisters were disappointed in Jesus. Mary's grief was worked out not through her beliefs but through her heart. As she knelt at Jesus' feet, weeping, her tears fell like prayers. Soon Jesus began to weep also.

This is one of the most hope-inspiring images of Jesus. God can be moved. Jesus was "greatly disturbed . . . and deeply moved" (11:33). Once we discover that God has joined our tears and can be moved with compassion, the world becomes a very unpredictable place. Who knows what may happen? That is the most important thing to recognize when Lazarus is dead. All that is left is our hope in a God who can be moved by how it is. And this is all we need.

Some commentators have suggested that Jesus began to weep because he knew that the answer to his earlier question, "Do you believe?" was "Not really." We believe that Jesus can help before death and loss, but not after. Apparently we believe that death is greater than Jesus.

The reason the gospel is such good news is that God is not limited even by our unbelief. Jesus stepped up to the cave in which his friend was buried and shouted, "Lazarus, come out!" As the formerly dead man emerged from the tomb, the Savior said, "Unbind him, and let him go" (11:43-44).

Like Lazarus, we who were abandoned by Jesus will also find this same life-creating power at work. Jesus does not create a new life for us because we believe. Who has that much belief? He creates something new because, only because, he loves us.

It can be frightening to receive that much salvation. To hear the Savior call us out from the dark cave of despair and grief can be startling if we have settled into that abandonment. For Christ to unbind us and set us free from the hurt we have wrapped around ourselves is dangerous, because we do not know where it will lead. If we cannot even count on death, then we live very unpredictable lives in an unpredictable world.

That is more hope than most of us want. According to John, it was at this point that the chief priests and Pharisees plotted to kill Jesus. If Jesus can defeat death, then nothing is certain. That may be too much mystery. We asked for a savior who would help us avoid death and give us what we want. When he comes, however, we discover we didn't really want God to get involved after all.

With God, change in our lives is inevitable, and without God, it is impossible. No matter how much we may want to change, until we see God differently we never will.

What Changes in Conversion?

I have been a pastor long enough to witness something of a pattern in Christian spiritual development. Like all patterns it is a generalization, and as with all generalizations, there are certainly exceptions. However, the pattern still attests to the common experience of many Christians.

In the beginning of the Christian life, people don't know so much. They just see Jesus and receive his grace. They are in love with him because they have discovered that he is in love with them. Like new lovers, they want to tell everybody what they have found. They are giddy with joy over what has happened to them, even though they are the first to admit how little they understand.

If new Christians are fortunate, there is a church that will bring them into the family and begin the long process of in-forming and shaping their faith. This is the second stage of their spiritual development. Before long they learn quite a bit. The church has spent two thousand years learning how to inculcate its beliefs, and it would make sense that we have become quite good at teaching converts what Christians believe. Eventually the disciples of Jesus acquire a lot of religious information. At some point, though, they realize this information is not reviving their souls. The old thirst for eternal water has returned. Although their heads are full of knowledge, their hearts have again become empty.

This propels Christians into the third stage, where they spend the rest of their lives—trying to get back to just seeing Jesus and receiving grace. They reach a point where they have participated in too many religious debates that all amount to how many angels can dance on the head of a pin. They have filled in the blanks of too many Bible study workbooks, and they have heard way too many Greek word studies from the pulpit. They have gone on too many mission work programs to have illusions about fixing the poor. They have seen too much of the church as a self-serving institution to still see it as the body of Christ. And one day it occurs to them that they have lost sight of Jesus.

That sets the agenda for the rest of their lives. It isn't that they drop out of church or stop learning. They just get intolerant of anything that doesn't help them get closer to Jesus. They are determined to find their passion for him once again. Now when they engage in mission, it is not to accomplish something, but in order to find Jesus in the places where they think he will be. If they read theology, it cannot simply fill their heads, but it must now inflame their hearts. The place where they worship can no longer be a school for saints, because now they have to check into a hospital for sinners where those who have wandered away from God can be restored and healed of their lonely diseases.

This is not a cynical commentary on Christian education, because the knowledge they have acquired is necessary. It is useful to the Spirit, who is determined to restore their vision of the Savior. The more knowledge they obtain and the more deeply they explore the truths of Scripture, the more humbled Christians become by God's great mystery. It is somewhat analogous to being married. I find that newly married couples assume too much familiarity with each other. When they argue, they say things like "You always do that." But I have overheard more than one old couple in our church say, "No kidding? I never knew that about you."

Confronted by the limitations of their knowledge, Christians experience even greater love for the God who never abandons them, even when they had worshiped the theologically constructed images of God that always abandoned them. It is at this third stage of development, when they have committed the rest of their lives to recovering a vision of Jesus, that they begin at long last to be converted into truly new creatures. This is not to say that there can be no change in a Christian's life at the beginning of the journey, but it is only an approximation of the miraculous transformation that is possible for those who have given up reading the Bible as if it were only an instruction manual for making changes on their own.

Early in the Christian journey we can easily change, but often that is little more than substituting one compulsion for another. People who craved power before they met Jesus quickly find positions of power in the church. People who once escaped from their problems in the culture of alcohol and drugs can now escape into the Christian subculture, where we offer a less destructive means of remaining numb and avoiding reality. It is an improvement, but we are essentially exchanging one set of addictions for another. People who were essentially nice before they really started their Christian journey are going to make nice Christians, and people who were jerks before they became Christians are now going to become jerks who learn a lot of theology.

It is not until we tire of the things we can do for ourselves in the Christian life that we will open ourselves to real conversion, which can be accomplished only by God. We will not open ourselves to that sacred activity until we give up controlling God through all of the information we have learned about him. But once all of that breaks down, and we discover God is mystery, we become open to mystery in our own lives as well.

At last we are ready for anything. We have given up on rearranging our sins, because we have given up on rearranging our image of God. We have confessed that we do not understand our God, much less ourselves. All we can say is "God be merciful to me, a sinner." Now we are ready to receive God's transformation of our lives.

I have seen the most compulsive people finally give up trying to get life right. They can't explain it, but it had something to do with giving up their worship of a demanding God. I have seen the smartest among us finally get to a point of rejoicing in their great ignorance because knowledge no longer keeps them from experiencing God. They tell me that joy was born out of the realization that God kept showing up in places beyond their theological boundaries. I have even seen jerks become compassionate because they gave up on their angry God after he clearly abandoned them. Now they can discover the God of mercy, who shapes and molds them into his merciful servants.

How this happened, when it happened, why it happened—they don't really have answers to these questions, and they don't really have much interest in asking them. They are too busy beholding the beauty of the Lord.

David said that the one thing he had learned to ask of the Lord was to spend his life in God's worship. All he now wanted was "to behold the beauty of the LORD and to inquire in his temple" (Psalm 27:4). Typically we Protestants have done better at the inquiring than at beholding the beauty of God. It is not an accident, though, that beholding God's beauty came first for David. If we never really see God in his mysterious beauty, we are destined to ask the wrong questions. If we have asked the wrong questions of God, we will certainly ask the wrong questions of ourselves.

There is never a time when we ask a question more wrong than when we ask ourselves if we have faith in God. C. S. Lewis said that when he asked himself if he had faith he began to lose it, for then he looked at his faith and not God. The best way to strengthen faith is not to scrutinize it, but to look at the One in whom we are trusting. Being too focused on faith is like trying to improve our vision by taking off our glasses and looking at them. The point is to look through them, not at them. When we look through the spectacles of faith, we discover the awe-inspiring, uncontrollable, maybe even frightening activity of God. Then we realize it was never our faith that saved and changed us, but rather the God we do not understand.

Christians Who Stop Believing

Tom was raised in a Christian home. He made a decision to become a Christian when he was twelve years old and was baptized in his Baptist church the next Sunday. He eventually became a leader in his youth group, sang in the church choir and surprised no one when he went to a Christian college, where he majored in biblical studies. During college Tom helped out in a local church youth group and seemed to have a special gift for working with teenagers. After graduating, he had several offers from churches and parachurch groups to help direct their youth ministries.

In his new job Tom experienced tremendous success by all measurable standards. The kids loved him, the parents appreciated him, and his youth group grew in numbers as well as spiritual maturity. He married his college sweetheart, who was devoted both to Tom and to the ministry that they shared. For ten years things seemed to be perfect.

One day Tom stunned his supervisor by saying that he was resigning. The supervisor braced for the worst. He asked, "Why?" when what he wanted to say was, "Have you sinned morally?" Tom smiled knowingly and said, "No, it isn't what you are thinking. It's worse. I don't know if I still believe everything I say. I'm no longer certain who God is, and I can't pretend." After a series of long theological debates with the supervisor, late-night conversations with his wife and an extended leave of absence from his work, Tom left the ministry and enrolled in an MBA program. There was no crisis in his life that precipitated this loss of faith. He just stopped believing.

After finishing his graduate training, Tom got a good job with a manufacturing plant and maintained loving commitments to his family. He was supportive of raising their children in a local congregation and continued to sit in worship with his wife, who became a leader in the church's ministry. Every Sunday the congregation would stand and recite the Apostles' Creed. Tom could never get through the opening line, "I believe in God."

He never got used to living without faith. If asked, he would say that he was searching for God or whatever it was that was at the bottom of his life. He was quite successful in his career but found little purpose or meaning in it. He did charitable work in the community, but it offered no hope for him or those he served. Many nights he would come home from work to read literature or philosophers or theologians or anyone who had an angle on the truth. For years the search continued, and he found nothing. Eventually he became emotionally and intellectually exhausted. He was tired of his doubts and tired of his search. As he explained to his wife, he had resigned himself to the fact that "there was nothing else out there."

A professional move took Tom and his family to a new community. Again he followed his wife to church. But this church was different. The preacher was a well-read, silver-haired pastor who had little need to rehearse worn-out Christian jargon from the pulpit. He spoke honestly about doubt and faith as if they were companions and not enemies. He easily quoted French existentialists but always ended his sermons with a passionate love for Jesus. Tom wondered what held this preacher together.

One Sunday morning the sermon text was from the sixth chapter of John. After Jesus had performed many miracles including the feeding of the five thousand and walking on water, a large crowd of disciples began to follow him. Then Jesus spoke some harder words about who he was and where he was heading. Most of the new followers began to complain because they could not understand him or his "difficult teachings," and so they left. Jesus then turned to the Twelve and asked, "Do you also wish to go away?" It was Peter who responded, "Lord, to whom can we go? You have the words of eternal life" (John 6:67-68). It was clear that the disciples did not understand those words any better than the crowd. They just knew there was nothing else.

Tom sat in the pew and began to weep. *So this is it,* he thought. His great search had ended not with an illuminating discovery but with a tired whisper. Instead of the intellectual breakthrough to God that he had sought for years, he now knew he would return to the faith simply because there was no place else to go.

Like Peter, Tom does not understand all of Jesus' words. He has plenty of doubts but chooses to live as if the words of Jesus are true because he does believe this is the only Savior he has. Also like Peter, Tom continues to follow this Savior he cannot fully understand. It has to be enough to simply follow.

After the wise preacher retired, I followed in his pulpit. It has been my joy to inherit the pastoral care he began in the lives of many, including Tom's family. Not long ago, Tom's wife approached me at the end of worship with tears of her own and said, "Guess who said the Apostles' Creed today."

I have breakfast with Tom from time to time. I very much enjoy our conversations because I like him a great deal and admire his integrity. I also get to watch how faith develops as a response to the silence of God.

The Silence of God

God is often silent when we prefer that he speak, and he interrupts us when we prefer that he stay silent. His ways are not our ways.

To live with the sacred God of creation means that we conduct our lives with a God who does not explain himself to us. It means that we worship a God who is often mysterious—too mysterious to fit our formulas for better living. It means that God is not our best friend, our secret lover or our good-luck charm. He is God.

The sacred can never be contained by our fervent prayers, our theological boxes or our great need to have someone on our side. God will not be leashed. He will not speak on command. For this reason, we often turn to other gods that are more manageable. Some look for the sacred in work or in relationships or in nature. Disillusioned with these, many have joined the faddish infatuation with the New Age movement. When we're tired of that, we will move on to something else that looks more promising. The problem is that our substitute gods do not satisfy us. That is because we have been created with a craving for the sacred. Nothing else will do.

It was the search for the sacred that drove Tom away from

the too-well-rehearsed answers that had been so much a part of his Christian background. He craved a relationship to something truly sacred, but all he had was a stale orthodoxy. If belief is nothing more than the right answers, it is not belief in God but in a religious system. It was the Pharisees' fervent commitment to religion that got Jesus so irritated at them. They too had all the right answers, but they did not love God.

Essentially, the Pharisees' problem, and ours, is in understanding the difference between knowing God and knowing *about* God.[1] We easily confuse the two. One implies information, while the other is a vital relationship. Historians can devote their lives to knowing all they can about Abraham Lincoln. They can study his life and writings, memorize verses of his speeches and argue with each other about the exact interpretation of his words. But in the end they cannot say they knew him. That is reserved for those who lived with the man. Typically Protestant churches are better at helping people know things about God than we are at helping them know God as people who live with him. It should come as no surprise that when Christians really need their faith, if knowledge is all they have, they will soon wander away in search of a God worth worshiping.

I would not say that Tom's journey is completely typical for Christians who stop believing. It is not always the case that the problem is primarily intellectual. Sometimes the crisis in faith is caused by a crisis in health or in a marriage. Maybe someone prayed and prayed for God to heal a loved one, but death came anyway—and it became impossible to believe that a loving God would let that happen. However the journey through doubt begins, the return to God is usually the same. Like the prodigal son, doubters don't come back to the Father's house because they have figured things out. Nor do they come home because the Father went after them. It's because after wandering around for a while doubters get tired and spent. Eventually they remember the place they left.

Anyone who has made that journey can attest to the fear and pain that it brings. However, it is not unique. Maybe in less dramatic ways we all have to make our way back to the Father's house because we all wander away. Maybe we don't wander away from our beliefs for many years, but we live as if they were not true. This is particularly tempting when belief is all that we have because God has not given us any miraculous signs of his presence. That is why confession is such an important part of the Christian journey. In these prayers we are essentially telling God that we got tired of not hearing the directions we wanted from him, wandered off on our own and now are very lost. But that is the beginning of the good news.

It is only the prodigals who find themselves in the arms of the Father. The elder brother who stays with the father undergoes no religious experience. It is very dangerous to our spiritual lives to live too carefully. In the words of Simone Weil, "there is no safe side to true belief."[2] If the prodigal had lived economically, he would never have had to find his way home to the father. The recurring reminders of how far we have roamed from God make us all the more ready to receive God's grace—which is the only way we get back home. The point of the parable, as the elder brother should have realized, is not to be right. The point is to get into the arms of the Father.

Throughout our absence from home, the Father waits, ready to receive those who are ready to return to his outstretched arms. "For thus says the high and lofty one who inhabits eternity, whose name is Holy: I dwell in the high and holy place, and also with those who are contrite and humble in spirit" (Isaiah 57:15).

"Jesus, Do You Care?"
The disciples were at sea with Jesus in their boat, when a great

storm blew in. The sky grew dark, and the waves started to crash into the boat. We can imagine the disciples frantically pulling down the sails and bailing out water as they tried to steer their small ship into the wind. Maybe they wondered how this storm could come up so quickly. Maybe they thought that as long as Jesus was in their boat, nothing could happen to them. But the storm worsened as Jesus slept in the captain's chair. He seemed to have abandoned his job as the captain of that storm-tossed ship.

As Mark tells the story (Mark 4:35-41), he builds the narrative around three important questions. The first question came from the disciples as they woke Jesus up: "Teacher, do you not care that we are perishing?"

We all know that question. The phone rings. It's bad news. A parent has died. A child's marriage is over. The tumor is malignant. As we hang up the phone, the sky grows dark. The winds begin to blow, and the waves of a great storm start to break into our little boat called life. "Jesus," we pray, "don't you care about this?" We know that Jesus is powerful. We have heard what he can do. Maybe we have seen something of his power in other people's lives. The question isn't "Jesus, can you do anything?" The question is "Jesus, do you care? Do you care about me?"

Jesus calms the storm and then asks the disciples a question of his own. "Why are you afraid? Have you still no faith?" Jesus expects us to know that faith does not insulate us from the storms. It has little to do with our doctrines or even with our belief that Jesus could come up with a miracle if he would only pay attention. Faith has everything to do with seeing that we have the Savior on board.

The disciples are filled with awe at what they have just seen. They have traveled with the "Teacher" for a long time. But now they know he is more than a teacher of insights and wisdom.

138

Even the wind and the sea obey him. They then ask the third question, which at some point has been echoed by every disciple since then. "Who is this man?" As in every good worship experience, they have moved from fear to reverence. The final question behind every miracle isn't "What can Jesus do?" but "Who is he?" Once we know who he is, the questions about miracles are not as interesting.

We doubt that Jesus will change the way it is in our lives or our world, because we think we know Jesus too well. We assume that he is just our teacher or our ticket to heaven or the busy Savior of the world who is too preoccupied to care about us. When we assume we know what Jesus will do, we assume we know what will happen in our lives when the storms hit. But there is mystery to the Savior. This brings mystery into our lives as well, because we do not know how he will intervene.

When I was in a college art appreciation class, I wrote a paper on the paintings of Sir Joshua Reynolds. I had spent a lot of time in the museum and had studied his work thoroughly, and I wanted to demonstrate my expertise to the professor. I filled the research paper with references to the mistakes Reynolds made in his portraits, the scratches that authenticated the original works and the "obvious" ways he used his students to paint the backgrounds of his portraits. When the professor returned my paper, her only comment was "But what did you think of his art?"

It is easy to discount the familiar and so lose sight of the mystery and genius in what we think we know so well. It is particularly hard to appreciate God's creativity in our own lives. We get so used to the scratches that we can't see the art. Whenever we domesticate the mysterious into something familiar, it abandons us.

When Jesus returned to Nazareth to preach, people kept

asking, "Isn't this Joseph and Mary's boy?" They thought they knew Jesus so well that they didn't get to know him at all. At the end of Jesus' life one of the thieves on the cross knew him much better than those who had spent years watching him grow up. If the people of Nazareth had been at Calvary, I imagine they still would have said, "Isn't that Joseph and Mary's boy?" They would have thought that the scars on his hands, his feet and his side were just ugly blemishes. What they would not have seen is that those were the marks of their salvation.

The Abandonment of Jesus

The Christian gospel turns on the events of Good Friday and Easter. Before the cross, the biblical story is about our abandonment of paradise and homeland and the Father's house. No matter how many times we reaffirmed our commitment to staying close to God this time, it was not long before we wandered away. Sometimes we left in search of other gods. Sometimes we grew impatient at following a Savior who kept talking about the exorbitant cost of being his disciple but never led us to the places we wanted to go. By the time the reader of the Bible makes it to the end of the Gospels, it is clear that we are not capable of staying with God. Thus we will continue to experience the abandonment of God, who will not go with us to the places where we keep getting lost in our search for another salvation. If we are to find God, it will only be as a result of his finding us. God will have to join in our abandonment.

Jesus' atonement for our sin on the cross is explained through many biblical images. As the Lamb of God, he paid the price for our disobedience. As the great high priest, he bridged the gulf that had been created between God and humanity. As the suffering servant, his passion embodied the God who is with those who suffer. All these theories of the atonement are absolutely right and deserve the detailed analysis they receive. There is another purpose to the atonement, though, which is equally significant. On the cross Jesus took on our godforsakenness.

The image of Jesus hanging on the cross asking his father, "Why hast thou forsaken me?" is one of Christianity's darkest moments. How could God the Father turn his back on the beloved Son? In spite of Jesus' resolve to be our sacrifice, how did the angels keep from rushing down heaven's ladder to save the only one who was at home with the Father? Some help is given by Paul's insight that "for our sake he made him to be sin who knew no sin, so that in him we might become the righteousness of God" (2 Corinthians 5:21). The Father abandoned Jesus on the cross because he had become our sin.

For reasons that are not clear to me, Christians today are not fond of this image of the atonement. Maybe we are uncomfortable with Jesus becoming our sin because we don't really believe our creeds that claim he was fully God and fully human. What we want to say is that he was fully God who looked like a human. We want a Jesus who fixes up our lives and teaches us insights as only a God can do. But we get nervous about the Word made flesh. That is a heresy as old as Gnosticism, and the church today can be no less tolerant of it than the early church was. There is no salvation if God only visited the earth for a while without ever becoming contaminated by our flesh. That line of thinking as always led to preoccupation with Jesus' moral teaching, which in turn has always led Christians to thinking of themselves as a spiritually elite corps who understand theological formulas. But I think our misgivings about the image of a forsaken Savior probably run deeper than this theological drifting.

Actually, our problem with this image is that it scares us to death. If God can turn his back on his Son, we assume he can turn his back on us. That is where we could not be more wrong. In fact, it is precisely because he abandoned his Son on the cross that we will never have to fear God turning away from us. For in turning away from Jesus made sin, the Father turned toward us who in that moment were made right, made "the righteousness of God."

How could such a dark, forsaken image be filled with so much hope? How could the Father love us so much that he would forsake his Son? Maybe that is what is so frightening. What really scares us to death is to receive that much love. But fear is exactly the right response if we are going to receive the new life that will come when we accept that extravagant love.

We call that grace—God giving us what we need, not what we deserve. It is a scandal. It was a scandal to heaven for Jesus to be sacrificed for a world filled with sinners. It is a scandal to those who have not yet confessed that all their righteousness is but filthy rags. Grace confronts us with the accusation that no matter how hard we try, we cannot save ourselves. That will come only by receiving the love of God.

If we do that, if we accept that love, everything changes. That is the price of accepting God's grace. Soon we will find that we too have turned our backs to the cross where our efforts at saving ourselves died. The time has come to face the risen Savior, who will now lead us into a new vocation of being with the Father forever.

The Unfinished Story
All four of the Gospels describe the resurrection, but in less detail than we would like. Mark's account is the shortest, and its ending seems almost abrupt. The original version of the Gospel probably ended with the angel speaking to the women inside Jesus' empty tomb. Knowing that they are looking for Jesus, the angel says, "He has been raised; he is not here. He

is going ahead of you to Galilee" (see 16:6-7). Amen.

That's no ending. It leaves too much up in the air. Why didn't Jesus wait for the disciples at the tomb? Why did he abandon them there? What happened later in Galilee? How did that final encounter change their lives? At this point we don't know.

These are not just academic questions. On this side of Easter we want to know more details about how this risen Jesus will change our lives as well. But according to Mark, the gospel is intent on leaving this story unfinished. That is because the story is completed in every disciple the risen Savior has gone to meet. There are so many chapters still to be written.

We already know the chapter about what happened during that long spell when it was hard to see Jesus, and we thought he had abandoned us. Maybe we can even tell some of the story about how the risen Savior found us, and how different he seemed. By faith, we believe there is still a chapter or two yet to be written that is filled with life-changing hope. Because now we know that Jesus is ahead of us, beckoning, waiting for us to arrive.

The Easter story has no ending because it was designed to lead us into our future with God. Easter can't have an ending. It is not about what is finished but about what has just begun— a future that is so mysterious only God could write it. No matter how great the abandonment, how severe the loss, even if it is the loss of Jesus himself that we grieve, the message of the angel is "Don't keep weeping in the tombs." Where will we find our risen hope? He has gone on ahead . . .

8
Doxology

ON THE OTHER SIDE OF ABANDONMENT, all of life becomes an expression of gratitude. The journey through loss was long and filled with pain. It cost us our lives. At the bottom of the abandonment, the only thing that was left was the love of God. But to be alone with the love of God is the only way to find life again.

From Whom All Blessings Flow

Our church, like many, sings the doxology every Sunday. As the ushers bring our offerings to God back up to the front of the church, the organ swells and the congregation stands and begins to joyfully sing,

Praise God from whom all blessings flow,
Praise him, all creatures here below,
Praise him above, ye heavenly hosts,
Praise Father, Son, and Holy Ghost.

We sing that song so often that it can become something of a liturgical black hole into which our minds disappear. But even if we are muttering the words absent-mindedly, we are still rehearsing our role as a thankful people. As the pastor, I get to stand in front of the congregation and watch them as they sing this song. I wonder what they are thinking about as they sing their thanks to God for all of life's blessings.

Do we really believe that all blessings flow from God? As the ushers hold the offerings of the people before God, someone has to be thinking, _Praise God? I have worked myself to a frazzle to get that money I'm giving the church._ But if we think the money we put in that plate was ours to give, we have missed the point of worship. All of life comes as a blessing from God, even the blessings we would rather not have received. What we are placing in the plate is only a symbol of the life that we would put in the plate if only it fit.

Either we believe life is something that must be achieved, or we believe life is something that can only be received. Once we start seeing this choice in the Bible, we find it on almost every page. Is God the Creator, or are we? Is Jesus the Savior, or are we? Does the Holy Spirit give wisdom, or are we smart enough on our own? We've got to choose. The Bible cautions us to choose carefully.

If we decide to work hard to achieve our own lives, we have good reason to worry. We know too many people who have lost their marriages, businesses and health to really believe it could never happen to us. We've seen too many things that are hard to call blessings. In our bravest moments we have to admit that just about any tragedy under the sun could visit us tomorrow. So if it is only up to us to do well, anxiety will be our constant companion.

Anxiety is that ever-present, churning fear that life may slip through our fingers. People who are anxious come to worship with their hands clutching tightly to things they believe they got for themselves and must work hard to keep. Their doxology is "Thanks, God, that I wasn't born in a Third World country. Thanks that I had the chance to make a life. Please, dear God, don't take it all away." But someday it will all go away. Someday we will have to let go of our work, health and children. Someday we will have to leave loved ones in God's arms.

Those who have been frantic to achieve their lives will greet that day with anguish. But when that day comes for those who have learned to receive life as a gift, they will give life back with hearts full of gratitude, thankful for the gifts they were permitted to hold for a while.

Lessons from the Nursing Home

At the end of what had been a very long week, I found myself driving to a local nursing home to lead a Communion service. It was the last thing I wanted to be doing.

The week had begun with three days at a denominational renewal meeting that had been disastrous. I got back to my office on Wednesday to an "in box" that was two and a half inches thick filled with letters from people who have great dreams for our church and wanted to say that we were not doing enough to get it right. I had missed so much work earlier in the week that my day off on Thursday had to be scrapped. Friday morning I had to step into a staff conflict. Sunday was fast on my tracks, and the sermon was a long way from being ready.

Friday afternoon I raced over to the nursing home to "take care of this commitment." In the car, I actually prayed for God to help me get through this thing so I could get back to work. Unbelievable.

After I held a brief service for ambulatory residents, a couple of elders went with me to take Communion to those who were too disabled to leave their rooms. It was then that I met my priest for that day, Mrs. Lucille Lins.

Mrs. Lins is almost blind and very hard of hearing. She has gradually become shut off from the world. Her health has slipped away, and now she is confined to a small room, having given up her house years ago. She has outlived her husband and close friends. Very few people in our church still remember her. She has lost almost everything but life itself.

It was a humble scene. I tried to be cheery. She said something I could not understand. It was clear that we were not going to have a profound conversation. I muttered through the words, "This is my body broken for you. This is my blood poured out for you." We fumbled with the Communion. I helped her shaking hands find the bread on the little tray I held in front of her. We spilled the juice on my slacks. *Just one more thing that isn't going right,* I thought to myself. I prayed briefly, gave her a pat on the back and said something about how much God loved her. As I got ready to leave, she surprised me by beginning to pray.

In a clear voice she said, "Thank you, God, for being so good to me. Thank you that I am not forgotten. Thank you for always loving me."

At last something had broken through my manic efforts at being the savior. Stunned, I dropped back into my chair. A long time of silence passed. I did not want to leave her because this was my first sacred moment all week, and I knew this woman had so much to teach me. This blind woman could see what I could not.

I have received so much, and for now I am still holding on to most of it. Mrs. Lins has lost everything but the love of God, and yet her heart is filled with gratitude. I had not prayed a single prayer of thanksgiving all week. I had been way too busy asking God to help me achieve more.

I slowly drove back to the church repeating the prayer I had just learned from this great saint. "Thank you, God, for being so good to me. Thank you that I am not forgotten. Thank you for always loving me." I can't imagine what would happen to Christians if we all prayed those words from the heart. We could stop trying so hard to become happy or successful or powerful. We would be too much in love with God to worry about those things. We could settle into the lives we have and love the real people God has given us, including those who do not deserve love—as if love were ever deserved. When you are loved, all you can do is be thankful.

The Vocation of Gratitude

"On the way to Jerusalem Jesus was going through the region between Samaria and Galilee. As he entered a village, ten lepers approached him" (Luke 17:11). It is striking that these people are identified only as ten lepers. We don't know a thing about their families or homes, their academic degrees, how successful they were before contracting leprosy, whether they were men or women. That is what the disease does to people. It takes away all distinguishing characteristics. We don't even know the names of these people. They are just "ten lepers." Beyond that, all we know is that one of them was a Samaritan. They were are all looking for mercy.

The first thing this text tells us about Christian vocation is that before any of us approach Jesus and offer to do something significant, we first have to see ourselves as one of the undistinguished lepers in search of his mercy. This first lesson may be the hardest. Most Christians want to be of service to God. However, we want to begin God's mission as relatively whole people with names and faces and distinctive stories that make us somebodies who deserve to be used. But the truth is that the diseases of life have left us all with crippled relationships, crippled dreams and crippled health. By the time we make it to Jesus, all that is left is our rather common need for mercy.

Graham Greene is one of my favorite authors. His novel *A Burnt Out Case* has been such a theologically rich resource for me that I've had to promise myself I would quote from it in my sermons only once a year. It's the story of an architect named Querry who built cathedrals but did not believe in God. Querry enjoyed fame and success, but no matter how great the cathedral he built, he could find no meaning to his life. Eventually he dropped out of society and headed to what he believed was the last place on earth—a leper colony in Congo, Africa. When Querry arrived, he told the doctor in charge that he was there because he belonged there. His soul has been eaten away.

It isn't long before Querry takes an interest in one of the patients, a crippled man named Deo Gratias. One day Deo Gratias wanders too far into the jungle. Querry goes to find him and gets lost himself. Late into the night the two find each other. "Deo Gratias raised a stump and howled, and Querry realized he was crippled with fear. The fingerless hand fell on Querry's arm like a hammer and held him there. There was nothing to do but wait for morning." The next day when Querry speaks to the doctor, he says, "Usually nights are when things come to an end in my life. But this was a new beginning. There wasn't a thing either of us could do, but hold on to each other in this clumsy embrace."[1]

With that clumsy embrace Querry begins his pilgrimage back to God. It is as if he has at long last embraced his true condition as a leper, and in doing so finds he is holding the glory of God. That night is the beginning of his conversion. Eventually he builds a very simple hospital for the colony. He considers it his life's masterpiece, because for the first time he has built something with gratitude and love.

Our mission of service to God can never, never begin by thinking we have something to offer. Certainly there are many things to give God: our time, talents, money, words of hope about the gospel. But we never begin there. We begin with the confession that whether we're a success or an outcast, we need mercy. Otherwise what we call Christian mission will actually be a disguise for remaining powerful. When we give charity to the needy and throw a quarter in the kettle, often it is just to feel good about ourselves. History has documented how dangerous missions can become on the global level when the sending churches throw money at the world's problems. That has proven disruptive to the Third World and deadly to the soul of wealthy Western churches. If we want to convert the world around us into a more holy place, we have to begin by allowing ourselves to be converted into lepers. Then we can join the voices of those who cry for mercy.

When Jesus saw the lepers, "he said to them, 'Go and show yourselves to the priests.' And as they went, they were made clean. Then one of them, when he saw that he was healed, turned back, praising God with a loud voice" (Luke 17:14). If the first lesson on mission is to turn toward our suffering, the second is to then turn back to Jesus Christ in thanksgiving.

All Christian mission is about gratitude for what Jesus has done in our own lives. Those who engage in Christian mission are not benevolent providers of charity. They are not theologically correct proselytizers. They are emissaries of gratitude.

I remember when as a young man it finally hit me that I was in love. The remarkable thing, the thing that took awhile to trust, was that I was loved by this woman. Falling in love is a way of expressing the heart's deep gratitude for receiving someone's love. Mission is simply what we find irresistible to do when we really believe that God loves us. It's an expression of gratitude, and thus a way of falling more deeply in love.

Whether it is the love we offer to our neighbors and colleagues or the love missionaries offer whole groups of people, whenever love enters the world, so does God. Because God is love.

It is fascinating that all ten of the lepers in Luke's story were healed from their disease. All of them received mercy, but only the Samaritan returned to give praise to his healer. Only the outsider was made part of the thankful fellowship. No matter how long we have been a part of that fellowship, no matter how many times we have stood to sing the doxology, we have to remember that by rights we do not belong in this house of the Lord. We were brought there by the mercy of Jesus.

Then Jesus said to him, "Get up and go on your way; your faith has made you well" (Luke 17:19). It is as we go on our way that we find it irresistible to talk about what has happened to us. But the faith we talk about is never reduced to convincing others of the validity of our theological formulas for salvation. That is not what saved us. What saved us was the mercy of Jesus. Like young people who have fallen in love, we want to talk about Jesus all the time. We couldn't stop talking about him if we tried. We are too much in love.

That is the basis of our ministry to others. It is a response to receiving the love of a Savior. Dr. Samuel Hines was a great pastor of Washington's inner city. For over twenty-five years he poured himself into the lives of the people in his congregation. Shortly before he died, I had the opportunity to talk with him about ministry in our city. I had arrived recently and was trying to provide some hope to the inner city. I had worked only long enough to get discouraged. Sam faced far greater obstacles than I. His church was poor, and the needs of his neighborhood were overwhelming. But I never saw him discouraged. As we sat in one of the pews of his humble church, I asked him what kept him going.

He laughed and said, "Ah, it has little to do with me. Craig, never forget all Christian mission is about gratitude for what God has done, is doing and is going to do." Our mission is to see the work of God and to love it. All we do for Jesus is essentially an expression of gratitude. That is the only well deep enough to supply our love for those around us.

Passionate Living

To love someone is to enter a passionate, dramatic journey with that person. We do not know where the love will take us. Typically it leads us to the heights and the depths of our lives. No one else can fill our hearts with such joy or break them apart with such hurt. That is exactly what happens to us when we offer compassion to others as an expression of our love for Jesus.

Every pastor I know has stories of being on emotional roller coasters that whisked them up to great heights of joy and then plunged them into low valleys of grief. A Saturday that begins with the celebration of a wedding may end with the funeral of a child or the sudden death of a family member in an automobile accident. Such events are the high drama of life.

More subtle drama occurs every day, but it is harder to see. That is because our preference for the safe middle ground in life makes us blind to the passion of real life. If we actually believed God was waiting for us at the higher and lower ends of life, we might not choose to settle into this middle ground where it is hard to see the drama of God, where the days are so gray. We might choose instead to venture out into the deeper colors of life that we are called to explore. Most Christians I know could use more passion in their lives. Most of us do not cry hard enough or laugh loudly enough. I think we avoid the drama because we are afraid of it.

We have been taught to live too much of life on the flat plane between the highs and lows, where we settle for reasonable expectations that starve the passion out of life. Most of us cannot remember the last time we soaked our pillow with tears because of something that happened to a neighbor, much less to a country in eastern Europe or Africa. Nor can we remember the last time we read a newspaper that had such good news in it we had to hug someone in joy that a little bit more of Christ's kingdom had broken into the world. Maybe that is because we are afraid of making fools of ourselves by letting our expectations of the world get too high. But Christians who have lost their lives following Jesus give up modest hopes. Being his disciple is much too dramatic for cautious living.

Jesus spent a lot of time at the high and low ends of life. As God in the flesh, Jesus lived with a passionate dream. It wasn't very realistic considering the options, but Jesus consistently peered beyond the reasonable possibilities to call people to a very dramatic life with God. When he saw a shriveled little tax collector do the impossible thing of giving half his money back to the poor, Jesus got so elated he threw a party at Zacchaeus's house. The impossible vision of God had just broken through everyone's expectations. When the Savior saw the temple defiled by those with no regard for holiness, he went crazy with anger and turned the place upside down. It made him furious to see humanity settle for a world without the sacred. But that is exactly what we do when we insist on a cautious life. God will not be contained by any of our expectations, least of all those that attempt to domesticate holiness into formulas that can be easily marketed.

Through a character in one of his novels, John Updike observes, "Westerners have lost whole octaves of passion. Third world women can still make an inhuman piercing grieving noise right from the floor of the soul."[2] The music of life gets pretty thin without the higher and lower octaves. It loses its interest and becomes dull and predictable. That is the great danger of living in a sophisticated society that assumes its technology and wealth have taken the risks out of life. Most middle-class Westerners do not live in the fear that their homes will be invaded by violence, starvation or attacking soldiers. These events exist only in books and in movies which use the subject to entertain us. But the reality is that beneath the thin veneer of our decent and orderly lives is more drama than we want to see.

Seldom does a week go by that I am not invited into the home of a family that has discovered just how vulnerable it is to the invasions of disease, death and broken promises. Often there have been deep problems in the home for a long time, but a conspiracy of silence developed that made it impossible to discuss the issue. It is as if everyone became partially deaf to the lower octave. Eventually the dark tones of pain grew so loud they could no longer be ignored, but by then it is usually too late to recover the balance the family once had.

Since we are afraid of venturing down into these lower octaves, we construct lives that also make it hard to listen to the moments of ordinary joy that occur constantly above us. There are so many reasons for praising God in the course of a day. But since we are rushing about so quickly trying to save our lives, we miss the more gentle sounds that cause even heaven to rejoice. "Look at the birds of the air; they neither sow nor reap nor gather into barns, and yet your heavenly Father feeds them. Are you not of more value than they?" (Matthew 6:26).

Not long after I left seminary, I took a group of college students from our church to a short-term work camp in Central America. After the first week of living and working with a small, impoverished church in the barrio, we became quite caught up in the issue of why God allowed such intense poverty to exist.

We discussed it every night in our Bible study. We talked about it often as we repaired holes in the roof of the old church, and almost always at meals. Our food was served to us by local women, who cared for us with great joy. We visited their small homes that were often little more than cardboard nailed over some discarded lumber. Even the young women looked old and bent from the harshness of their lives. We would soon be leaving that wretched place, but these women and their beautiful children would probably never leave. The hard part was knowing that the children with whom we played every night would almost certainly grow into a life that was no better than the one eked out by their parents.

One night at dinner we asked the pastor of the church to give us his perspective on how Christians proclaim hope to those who live with such despair. While we asked our questions, we could hear the voices the women who were cooking for us through the thin walls of the kitchen. The pastor seemed surprised by the question. He said it was clear that his people were poor and probably always would be. "But despair?" he asked. "Where have you seen despair here?" At that moment, we heard laughter from the kitchen. We looked up to see the women watching a young boy juggle oranges. "Is that the sound of despair?" the pastor asked. "Jesus Christ is our Savior. How could we despair as those who have no hope?" As he spoke, I thought back to our own new church kitchen, which had been the subject of many arguments as one group fought with another about control and responsibility for that coveted piece of church turf. I couldn't imagine our members even allowing a child in the kitchen, much less enjoying him to the point of laughter. But these women took such joy at a boy juggling oranges. It turned our thoughts around. We spent the rest of the trip talking about why our middle-class lifestyles tempt us to despair with a future that seemed even more predictable than the one in the barrio.

It is not hard for me as a pastor to raise money for the poor, construct programs that care for them or even to get people to hand out food and blankets to the homeless. But that is not the mission of Jesus Christ, who typically developed a relationship with those in need. That is what is hard for the church. We would rather objectify the poor into an issue. Then we can argue the politics or theologies of the left and right to find solutions to these issues. But if we discover that the poor have names and faces and stories that will break our hearts, we do more than argue issues. Then we have to evaluate our own lives as well.

If we are going to stay with Jesus, we will have to tell the truth about our own need for his salvation. Soon we are back to the cross, where his passion always leads. That is too much passion for most of us.

Gratitude for God's Creation
There is an enormous effort in many churches today to help people become what we think they need to be. Usually this means to make them into something other than what they are. To no small degree this effort is fueled by the great dissatisfaction people have with their lives and their great fears that they are stuck with themselves until they die. This anxiety leads them into a thousand different expressions of what is essentially a yearning to become something else. Trying to stay competitive in the self-help market, the church often promises that if we just follow Jesus he will convert us into new creations. What we mean by that and what the Bible means are not necessarily the same.

When God converts us, he does not give us a new identity; rather, he allows us to discover what our true identity has been all along. The difference is very significant. As we make our way through the many abandonments of life and discover the new life that God is continuing to create, we realize that this new life does not look totally strange to us. What it looks like is a purer form of ourselves. It is the self we were created to be from the beginning. It is the restoration of the image of God in our lives. It is a reflection of the very image of Jesus Christ. But it is not something different from the good creation God had in mind for us from the beginning.

We certainly do not create our own lives. God alone is our creator. So why would his work of conversion in our lives result in something different from what he has intended for us all along? The saving work of Jesus Christ is that he finds us after we have lost our way trying to become something other than we are. Our churches would do better to stand in the way of the illusion that religion or anything else is going to help us *become something*. Instead we need the churches to help us to *be who we are*.

Those who understand this live with gratitude. These are the great saints of the church. They are of great use to the ministry of Jesus Christ because they are not preoccupied with making something of themselves. They have died to that, over and over again, until at last they can accept the great beauty of who they are. After a lifetime of losing their lives, mature saints of God have found someone who is fallible, alone and riddled with imperfections by every standard our world maintains. But that is the creature that God made and called "good." And a saint will no longer call it "not good enough." That is because every saint's first and last duty in this life is simply to give praise to God.

The Shorter Catechism asserts, "Man's chief end is to glorify God, and to enjoy him forever." We cannot enjoy God unless we live to glorify him. We cannot do that as long as we are trying to improve on the creation we have received.

When we truly enjoy God, we become free to enjoy the world around us. Our children are no longer perceived as imperfect objects that we need to change into our own image of goodness. Our friends and spouses are no longer manipulated into being what we need from them. The backgrounds in which we were raised no longer become something that we have to flee in order to find ourselves. Our mission work among the poor and our evangelism among those who do not know Christ as Lord are no longer frustrated by the idolatrous need to fix things.

This is not to say that all sorts of changes may not need to occur in our relationships or in the world around us. That is why we are converted for and by the mission Christ gives us. However, if our starting place for mission is joyful gratitude for what God has done and is doing and is going to do, we are less likely to take over as anxious substitutes for the Creator.

People who have a God do not need to become one. They are too consumed with watching the Lord's salvation unfold. Ask the saints, and they will tell you. There is nothing as joyful as witnessing the salvation of the Lord.

Notes

Chapter 1: Losing Our Lives
[1]Alan Jones, *Sacrifice and Delight: Spirituality for Ministry* (New York: HarperCollins, 1992), p. 97.

[2]The Gallup survey was completed in preparation for the 1992 presidential election. *Wisconsin State Journal,* September 13, 1992, p. 1.

[3]William J. Bennett, *The Index of Leading Cultural Indicators: Facts and Figures on the State of American Society* (New York: Touchstone, 1994), pp. 51, 55, 58.

[4]Jacques Ellul, *Hope in Time of Abandonment* (New York: Seabury, 1973), p. 8.

Chapter 3: A Place You'd Rather Not Go
[1]Henri Nouwen, commencement address, Princeton Theological Seminary, June 2, 1981. See Nouwen, "A Place You'd Rather Not Go," *Princeton Seminary Bulletin* 3, no. 3 (1982): 237.

[2]Ibid., p. 238.

[3]Margaret Farley, *Personal Commitments,* as quoted in Lewis Smedes, *Caring and Commitment* (San Francisco: Harper & Row, 1988), p. 39.

Chapter 4: Abandoned by Success
[1]H Richard Niebuhr, "The Responsibility of the Church for Society," in *The*

Gospel, the Church and the World, ed. Kenneth Scott Latourette (New York: Harper, 1946), p. 120.

Chapter 5: Abandoned by Health
[1]C. S. Lewis, *The Great Divorce* (New York: Macmillan, 1946), pp. 98-105.

Chapter 6: Abandoned by Family
[1]For a thorough study of the differences between what we now call the "traditional family" and the biblical images of family, see Rodney Clapp, *Families at the Crossroads: Beyond Traditional and Modern Options* (Downers Grove, Ill.: InterVarsity Press, 1993).

[2]Dietrich Bonhoeffer, *Life Together* (San Francisco: Harper & Row, 1954), p. 26.

[3]Anne Lamott, *Operating Instructions* (New York: Fawcett Columbine, 1993), p. 210.

Chapter 7: Abandoned by God
[1]J. I. Packer, *Knowing God* (Downers Grove, Ill.: InterVarsity Press, 1973), p. 25.

[2]Simone Weil, *Waiting for God* (New York: Putnam's, 1951), p. 5.

Chapter 8: Doxology
[1]Graham Greene, *A Burnt Out Case* (London: Penguin, 1960), p. 57.

[2]John Updike, *Roger's Version* (New York: Alfred A. Knopf, 1986), p. 273.